THE GRASS
GROWS BY ITSELF

THE GRASS GROWS BY ITSELF

Bhagwan Shree Rajneesh talks on Zen

Compilation:
Swami Anand Devesh

Editing:
Ma Prem Veena

RAJNEESH FOUNDATION · POONA · INDIA

Copyright by
Rajneesh Foundation
Poona, India

Published by
Ma Yoga Laxmi
Rajneesh Foundation
Shree Rajneesh Ashram
17 Koregaon Park
Poona 411 001, India

Printed by
DeVorss & Company, Publishers
P.O. Box 550
Marina del Rey, California 90291

First Clothbound Edition
December 1976
Printed in India

First Paperback Edition January 1978
Second Paperback Printing April 1979
Printed in the United States of America

Acknowledgement is given to the following
for the stories used in this book:

Zen Buddhism — *Peter Pauper Press*
Zen: Poems, Prayers, Sermons, Anecdotes, Interviews
    Ed. Stryk and Ikemoto — *Doubleday*
Zen Flesh, Zen Bones P. Reps — *Pelican*

THE GRASS GROWS BY ITSELF
is a series of eight talks on Zen. They were given by
Bhagwan Shree Rajneesh at his ashram in Poona, India,
and were recorded early in 1975.

BHAGWAN SHREE RAJNEESH

>   Sitting silently
>   Doing nothing
>   Spring comes
>   And the grass grows by itself.

These are the words of the ancient Zen Master, Zenerin. And they have come to be a refrain which now plays constantly through my being when I feel the presence of another Zen Master, my Zen Master, Bhagwan Shree Rajneesh.

For me, the main significance of the refrain is two-fold.

Firstly, this is Bhagwan—no words could more aptly describe what he is about. All day he sits in his room and does nothing—which gives rise among his sannyasins to a number of humorous quips about the 'trials' of enlightenment: 'You don't get to do anything, go anywhere, see anyone—must be a bit of a drag!' But that is only a joke because all the time we are aware, albeit very dimly, of the most incredible range and vastness of what is happening as a result of his silence and non-doing.

Secondly, a Master's being is his 'teaching'—the word is used only for want of a better one. Our total education has been to do, to act, to achieve, to stick as many fingers into the pie as possible. Hence the disaster that is us! From Bhagwan's being streams the constant message: let-go—stop doing, stop acting, stop achieving, stop meddling in this beautiful, divine existence; because it is the very meddling that is the cause of all our miseries. Without the meddling, all that we have been meddling so hard about happens.

From the Zen story 'The Cataract at Luliang' come the lines:

> *I go in with the whirl and come out with the swirl.*
> *I accommodate myself to the water, not the water to me.*

This is Bhagwan's Zen, not Zen as tradition knows it—although the spirit of Buddha, of Lao Tzu, of the great Japanese Masters, breathes as deeply through it—but Bhagwan's Zen.

It is Zen because there are no rules, no rituals, no disciplines for the disciple to follow—the essence is non-doing, non-being. And it is Zen because the Master's techniques for helping his disciples to grow are 'shock' ones! As yet, Bhagwan has not been known to throw anyone out of a window or to punch anyone on the nose; his 'shocks' and the growth situations he creates for us are a bit more subtle—but still they are Zen-like.

It is Bhagwan, because. . . . This is the most difficult part to write. To say he is 'nothing', or Enlightened, or Divine, would be the truth—because that is what he says he is—but it is not honest on my part because I don't know what all that means. All I can say is something fairly hackneyed, but it is true for me where I am now, and that is: it is Bhagwan, because Bhagwan can meet the intellectually mature, but spiritually practically unborn Westerner, on absolutely his own ground; and he works with us not on the basis of a tradition, but on the basis of who, what, and where we are, now.

And if you should happen to come here and stay around for a little while, you will begin to notice that in the apparent silence, in the apparent nothingness, in the apparent lack of action, a happening so vast as to be almost inconceivable is taking place. Something—and a lot of it—is growing.

Ma Prem Veena

CONTENTS

1. **The Significance of Zen** — 1
   ....Bokuju answered:
   We dress, we eat.

2. **Master and Disciple** — 35
   ....Sitting silently, the spring comes,
   and the grass grows by itself.

3. **Emptiness and the Monk's Nose** — 65
   ....Thereupon, Sekkyo seized the monk's nose
   and gave it a great yank.

4. **The Cataract at Luliang** — 99
   ....No, replied the man, I have no way;
   plunging in with the whirl, I come out with the swirl.
   I accommodate myself to the water, not the water to me.
   And so I am able to deal with it after this fashion.

5. **The 'Master of Silence'** — 127
   ....To sell his humbug Zen
   he had two eloquent attendant monks
   to answer questions for him—
   but, as if to show his inscrutable silent Zen,
   he himself never uttered a word.

6. **Awakening** — 157
   ....At last he admitted failure
   and, determined to end it all,
   he went to the railing and slowly lifted his leg over it.
   At that very instant he had an awakening.

7. **Not a Dead One** — 187
   ....What happens to a man of enlightenment
   after death?

8. **A Field Dyed Deep Violet** — 213
   ....The mind which treats me
   to nothing is the original void—
   a delicacy of delicacies.

   Book List — 240

   Centre List — 242

The Significance of Zen
21st February 1975

*Somebody asked the master, Bokuju:
we have to dress and eat every day—
how do we get out of all that?*

*Bokuju answered:
We dress, we eat.*

*The questioner said:
I don't understand.*

*Bokuju answered:
If you don't understand,
put on your clothes and eat your food.*

What is Zen?
Zen is a very extraordinary growth.
Rarely does such a possibility become an actuality
because many hazards are involved.
Many times before, the possibility had existed—
a certain spiritual happening could have grown
and become like Zen
but it was never realised to its totality.
Only once in the whole history of human consciousness
has a thing like Zen come into being.
It is very rare.

So first I would like you to understand what Zen is,
because unless you do that these anecdotes won't be much help.
You need to know the complete background.
In that background, in that context,
these anecdotes become luminous—
suddenly you attain
to the meaning and the significance of them,
otherwise they are separate units.
You can enjoy them; sometimes you can laugh at them;
they are very poetic;
in themselves they are beautiful, unique pieces of art,
but just by looking at these anecdotes you will not be able
to penetrate into the significance of what Zen is.

So first try to follow me
slowly through the growth of Zen—how it happened.
Zen was born in India, grew in China, and blossomed in Japan.
The whole situation is rare.
Why did it happen that it was born in India,
but could not grow here and had to seek a different soil?
It became a great tree in China, but could not blossom there,
it had to again seek a new climate, a different climate—
and in Japan it blossomed like a cherry tree,
in thousands of flowers.
It is not coincidental, it is not accidental,
it has deep inner history.
I would like to reveal it to you.

India is an introvert country, Japan is extrovert,
and China is just in the middle of these two extremes.
India and Japan are absolute opposites.
So how come the seed was born in India
and blossomed in Japan? They are opposites;
they have no similarities; they are contradictory.
And why did China come just in the middle, to give soil to it?

A seed is an introversion.
Try to understand the phenomenon of the seed, what a seed is.
A seed is not outgoing; a seed has really turned upon itself.
A seed is an introvert phenomenon,
it is centripetal—the energy is moving inwards.
That's why it is a seed, covered and closed
from the outer world completely. In fact

The Significance of Zen

a seed is the loneliest, most isolated thing in the world.
It has no roots in the soil, no branches in the sky;
it has no connection with the earth,
no connection with the sky.
In fact it has no relationships around it.
A seed is an absolute island, isolated, caved in.
It does not relate.
It has a hard shell around it, there are no windows, no doors;
it cannot go out and nothing can come in.

Seed is natural to India.
The genius of India can produce seeds
of tremendous potentiality, but cannot give them soil.
India is an introverted consciousness.

India says the outer doesn't exist and even if it exists
it is of the same stuff that dreams are made of.
The whole genius of India has been trying
to discover how to escape from the outer,
how to move to the inner cave of the heart,
how to be centred in oneself,
and how to come to realise
that the whole world that exists outside consciousness
is just a dream—
at the most beautiful, at the worst a nightmare;
whether beautiful or ugly, in reality, it is a dream,
and one should not bother much about it. One should awake,
and forget the whole dream of the outer world.

The whole effort of Buddha, Mahavir, Tilopa, Gorakh, Kabir,
their whole effort through the centuries,
has been how to escape from the wheel of life and death:
how to enclose yourself,
how to completely cut yourself from all relationships,
how to be unrelated, detached,
how to move in and to forget the outer.
That's why Zen was born in India.

Zen means *dhyan*.
Zen is a Japanese change of the word *dhyan*.
Dhyan is the whole effort of Indian consciousness.
Dhyan means to be so alone, so into your own being,
that not even a single thought exists.
In fact, in English, there is no direct translation.

Contemplation is not the word.
Contemplation means thinking, reflection.
Even meditation is not the word
because meditation involves an object to meditate upon;
it means something is there.
You can meditate on Christ, or you can meditate on the cross.
But *dhyan* means to be so alone that there is nothing
to meditate upon. No object, just simple subjectivity exists—
consciousness without clouds, a pure sky.

When the word reached China it became *ch'an*.
When *ch'an* reached Japan, it became Zen.
It comes from the same Sanskrit root, *dhyan*.

India can give birth to *dhyan*.
For millennia the whole Indian consciousness
has been travelling on the path of *dhyan*—
how to drop all thinking
and how to be rooted in pure consciousness.
With Buddha the seed came into existence.
Many times before also, before Gautam Buddha,
the seed came into existence,
but it couldn't find the right soil so it disappeared.
And if the seed is given to the Indian consciousness
it will disappear, because the Indian consciousness
will move more and more inwards,
and the seed will become smaller and smaller and smaller,
until a moment comes when it becomes invisible.
A centripetal force makes things smaller, smaller, smaller—
atomic—until suddenly they disappear.
Many times before Gautam Buddha the seed was born—
Gautam Buddha was not the first to meditate
and to become a *dhyani,* to become a great meditator.
In fact he is one of the last of a long series.
He himself remembers twenty-four Buddhas before him.
Then there were twenty-four Jain Teerthankers,
and they all were meditators.
They did nothing else,
they simply meditated, meditated, meditated,
and came to a point where only they were,
and everything else disappeared, evaporated.

The seed was born

The Significance of Zen

with Parasnath, with Mahavir, Neminath, and others,
but then it remained with the Indian consciousness.
The Indian consciousness can give birth to a seed,
but cannot become the right soil for it.
It goes on working in the same direction
and the seed becomes smaller and smaller,
molecular, atomic, and disappears.
That's how it happened with the Upanishads;
that's how it happened with the Vedas;
that's how it happened with Mahavir and all others.

With Buddha it was also going to happen.
Bodhidharma saved him.
If the seed had been left with the Indian consciousness
it would have dissolved. It would never have sprouted,
because a different type of soil is needed for sprouting—
a very balanced soil.
Introversion is a very deep imbalance, it is an extreme.

Bodhidharma escaped with the seed to China.
He did one of the greatest things
in the history of consciousness:
he found the right soil
for the seed that Buddha had given to the world.

Buddha himself is reported to have said:
My religion will not exist for more than 500 years,
then it will disappear.
He was aware that it always happened that way.
The Indian consciousness goes on grinding it
into smaller and smaller and smaller pieces,
then a moment comes
when it becomes so small that it becomes invisible.
It is simply no longer part of this world;
it disappears into the sky.

Bodhidharma's experiment was great.
He looked all around the world and observed deeply
for a place where this seed could grow.

China is a very balanced country, not like India,
not like Japan. The golden mean is the path there.
Confucian ideology is to remain always in the middle:
neither be introvert, nor be extrovert;

neither think too much of this world,
nor too much of that world—just remain in the middle.
China has not given birth to a religion, just morality.
No religion has been born there;
the Chinese consciousness cannot give birth to a religion.
It cannot create a seed.
All the religions that exist in China
have been imported, they have all come from the outside;
Buddhism, Hinduism, Mohammedanism, Christianity—
they have all come from the outside.
China is a good soil but it cannot originate any religion,
because to originate a religion
one has to move into the inner world.
To give birth to a religion
one has to be like a feminine body, a womb.

The feminine consciousness is extremely introvert.
A woman lives in herself;
she has a very small world around her,
the most minimum possible. That is why
you cannot interest a woman in things of great vastness. No.
You cannot talk about Vietnam to her, she doesn't bother.
Vietnam is too far away, too outer.
She is concerned with her family, her husband,
the child, the dog, the furniture, the radio set, the TV.
A very small world is around her, just the minimum.
Because she doesn't have a very big world around
it is very difficult for man and woman to talk intelligently—
they live in different worlds.
A woman is beautiful only when she keeps quiet;
the moment she starts talking then stupid things
come out of her. She cannot talk intelligently;
she can love, but she cannot talk intelligently.
She cannot be very philosophic, no, that's not possible.
These things are too far away, she doesn't bother.
She lives in the very small circle of her own world,
and she is the centre. And whatsoever is meaningful
is meaningful only in concern to herself—
otherwise it is not meaningful.
She cannot see why you are bothered about Vietnam.
What is the matter with you?
You are not related to the Vietnamese at all.

The Significance of Zen

Whether there is a war happening or not,
it is no concern of yours.
And the child is ill and you are bothering about Vietnam!
She cannot believe that she is present near you
and you are reading the newspaper.

Women live in a different world.
A woman is centripetal, introvert. All women are Indian—
wherever they are it makes no difference.
Man is centrifugal, he goes out.
The moment he can find an excuse he will escape from the home.
He comes to the home only when he cannot go anywhere else;
when all the clubs and hotels are closed, then, what to do?
He comes back home. Nowhere to go, he comes home.

A woman is always home-centred, home based.
She goes out only when it is absolutely necessary,
when she cannot do otherwise.
When it has become an absolute necessity she goes out.
Otherwise she is home based.

Man is a vagabond, a wanderer.
The whole of family life is created by women, not by men.
In fact, civilisation exists because of woman,
not because of man.
If he is allowed he will be a wanderer—
no home, no civilisation.
Man is outgoing, woman is ingoing;
man is extrovert, woman is introvert.
Man is always interested in something other than himself,
that's why he looks more healthy.
Because when you are too concerned with yourself,
you become ill. Man is more happy looking.

You will always find women sad and too concerned
with themselves. A little headache,
and they are very concerned, because they live inside—
the headache becomes something big, out of proportion.
But a man can forget the headache,
he has too many other headaches.
He creates so many headaches around himself
that there is no possibility
of coming upon his own headache and making something out of it.
It is always so little he can forget about it.

A woman is always concerned
—something is happening in the leg, something in the hand,
something in the back, something in the stomach,
always something—
because her own consciousness is focused inwards.
A man is less pathological, more healthy, more out-going,
more concerned about what is happening to others.

That's why, in all religions,
you will find that if there are five persons present,
four will be women, and one a man.
And that one man may have only come because of some woman—
the wife was going to the temple so he had to go with her.
Or, she was going to listen to a talk on religion,
so he came with her.
In all churches this will be the proportion,
in all churches, temples, wherever you go.
Even with Buddha this was the proportion,
with Mahavir this was the proportion.
With Buddha there were fifty thousand *sannyasins*—
forty thousand women and ten thousand men. Why?

Physically, man can be more healthy,
spiritually, woman can be more healthy,
because their concerns are different.
When you are concerned with others you can forget your body,
you can be more physically healthy,
but religiously you cannot grow so easily.
Religious growth needs an inner concern.
A woman can grow very, very easily into religion,
that path is easy for her,
but to grow in politics is difficult.
And for a man to grow in religion is difficult.
Introversion has its benefits; extroversion has its benefits—
and both have their dangers.

India is introvert, a feminine country;
it is like a womb, very receptive.
But if a child remains in the womb
for ever and for ever and for ever,
the womb will become the grave.
The child has to move out from the mother's womb,
otherwise the mother will kill the child inside.

He has to escape, to find the world outside,
a greater world.
The womb may be very comfortable—it is!
Scientists say we have not yet been able
to create anything more comfortable than the womb.
With so much scientific progress
we have not made anything more comfortable.
The womb is just a heaven.
But even the child has to leave that heaven
and come outside the mother. Beyond a certain time
the mother can become very dangerous. The womb can kill,
because it will then become an imprisonment—
good for a time, when the seed is growing,
but then the seed has to be transplanted to the outside world.

Bodhidharma looked around, watched the whole world,
and found that China had the best soil;
it was just a middle ground, not extreme.
The climate was not extreme, so the tree could grow easily.
And it had very balanced people.
Balance is the right soil for something to grow:
too cold is bad, too hot is bad.
In a balanced climate, neither too cold nor too hot,
the tree can grow.

Bodhidharma escaped with the seed,
escaped with all that India had produced.
Nobody was aware of what he was doing,
but it was a great experiment.
And he proved right.
In China, the tree grew, grew to vast proportions.

But, although the tree became vaster and vaster,
no flowers grew. Flowers did not come,
because flowers need an extrovert country.
Just as a seed is introvert, so a flower is extrovert.
The seed is moving inwards; the flower is moving outwards.
The seed is like feminine consciousness;
the flower is like male consciousness.
The flower opens to the outer world
and releases its fragrance to this outside world.
Then the fragrance moves on the wings of the wind
to the farthest possible corner of the world.

To all directions, the flower releases the energy
contained in the seed. It is a door.
Flowers would like to become butterflies
and escape from the tree.
In fact, that is what they are doing, in a very subtle way.
They are releasing the essence of the tree,
the very meaning, the significance of the tree, to the world.
They are great sharers.
A seed is a great miser, confined to himself,
and a flower is a great spendthrift.

Japan was needed. Japan is an extrovert country.
The very style of life and consciousness is extrovert.
Look...in India nobody bothers about the outside world
very much: about clothes, houses, the way one lives.
Nobody bothers. That is why India has remained so poor.
If you are not worried about the outside world,
how can you become rich?
If there is no concern to improve the outside world
you will remain poor.
And India is always very serious,
always getting ready to escape from life,
with Buddhas talking about how to become perfect drop-outs
from existence itself—not only from society,
ultimate drop-outs from existence itself!
The existence is too boring.
For the Indian eye, life is just a grey colour—
nothing interesting in it, everything just boring, a burden.
One has to carry it somehow, because of past karmas.
Even if an Indian falls in love
he says it is because of past karmas,
one has to pass through it.
Even love is like a burden one has to drag.

India seems to be leaning more towards death than life.
An introvert has to lean towards death.
That's why India has evolved all the techniques
of how to die perfectly,
of how to die so perfectly that you are not born again.
Death is the goal, not life.
Life is for fools, death is for those who are wise.
Howsoever beautiful a Buddha, a Mahavir may be,
you will find them closed;

around them a great aura of indifference exists.
Whatsoever is happening, they are not concerned at all.
Whether it happens this way or that way makes no difference;
whether the world goes on living, or dies,
it makes no difference...
a tremendous indifference.
In this indifference flowering is not possible;
in this inner-confined state, flowering is impossible.

Japan is totally different.
With the Japanese consciousness it is as if
the inner doesn't exist, only the outer is meaningful.
Look at Japanese dresses.
All the colours of flowers and rainbows—
as if the outer is very meaningful.
Look at Indian dresses, of the ancient days,
and look at the Japanese.
Look at an Indian when he is eating,
and look at the Japanese.
Look at an Indian when he takes his tea—and the Japanese.

A Japanese creates a celebration out of simple things.
Taking tea, he makes it a celebration. It becomes an art.
The outside is very important;
clothes are very important,
relationships are very important.
You cannot find more out-going people in the world
than the Japanese—always smiling and looking happy.
For the Indian they will look shallow;
they will not look serious.
Indians are the introvert people
and the Japanese are the extrovert:
they are opposites.

A Japanese is always moving in society.
The whole Japanese culture is concerned
with how to create a beautiful society,
how to create beautiful relationships
—in everything, in every minute thing—
how to give them significance.
Their houses are so beautiful.
Even a poor man's house has a beauty of its own;
it is artistic, it has its own uniqueness.

It may not be very rich,
but still it is rich in a certain sense—
because of the beauty, the arrangement,
the mind that has been brought to every small, tiny detail:
where the window should be,
what type of curtain should be used,
how the moon should be invited from the window, from where.
Very small things, but every detail is important.

With the Indian nothing matters.
If you go to an Indian temple, it is without any windows;
there is nothing,
no hygiene, no concern with air, ventilation—nothing.
Even temples are ugly,
and anything goes—dirt, dust, nobody bothers.
Just in front of the temple you will find cows sitting,
dogs fighting, people praying. Nobody bothers.
No sense of the outer,
they are not at all concerned with the outer.

Japan is very concerned with the outer—
just at the other extreme.
Japan was the right country.
And the whole tree of Zen was transplanted in Japan,
and there it blossomed, in thousands of colours.
It flowered.

This is how it has to happen again.
I am again talking about Zen.
It has to come back to India because the tree has flowered,
and the flowers have fallen and Japan cannot create the seed.
Japan cannot create the seed: it is not an introvert country.
So everything has become an outer ritual now.
Zen is dead in Japan.
It did flower in the past, but now, if by reading in books
—reading D.T. Suzuki and others—
if you go to Japan in search of Zen,
you will come back empty-handed.
Now Zen is here; in Japan it has disappeared.
The country could help it to flower,
but now the flowers have disappeared, fallen to the earth,
and nothing is there any more.
There are rituals—the Japanese are very ritualistic—

The Significance of Zen

rituals exist.
Everything in Zen monasteries is still continued the same way,
as if the inner spirit is still there,
but the inner shrine is vacant and empty.
The master of the house has moved.
The God is there no more—just empty ritual.
And they are extrovert people, they will continue the ritual.
Every morning they will get up at five
—there will be a gong—
they will move to the tea-room, and they will take their tea;
they will move to their meditation hall,
and they will sit with closed eyes.
Everything will be followed exactly as if the spirit is there,
but it has disappeared.
There are monasteries, there are thousands of monks,
but the tree has flowered and seeds cannot be created there.

Hence I am talking so much about Zen here—
because again only India can create the seed.
The whole world exists in a deep unity, in a harmony—
in India the seed can again be given birth.
But now many things have changed around the world.
China is no longer a possibility,
because it has itself become an extrovert country.
It has become communistic:
now matter is more important than the spirit.
And now it is closed for new waves of consciousness.

To me, if any country
can in the future become again the soil,
it is England.

You will be surprised, because you may think it is America.
No. Now the most balanced country in the world is England,
just as in the ancient days it was China.
The seed has to be taken to England and planted there;
it will not flower there, but it will become a big tree.
English consciousness
—conservative, always following the middle way,
the liberal mind, never moving to the extremes,
just remaining in the middle—
will be helpful.
That is why I am allowing more and more English people

to settle around me. It is not only for visa reasons!
Because, once the seed is ready,
I would like them to take it to England.
And from England it can go to America,
and it will have a flowering there,
because America is the most extrovert country right now.

I tell you that Zen is a rare phenomenon,
because only if all these situations are fulfilled
can such a thing happen.

Now, try to understand the story.
These small anecdotes are very meaningful,
because Zen people say
that that which arises in the depth of your being
cannot be said, but it can be shown.
A situation can be created in which it can be hinted at,
words may not be able to tell anything about it,
but an alive anecdote can.
That is why Zen is so anecdotal.
It lives in parables, indicates in parables, and nobody else
has been able to create such beautiful parables.
There are Sufi stories, there are Hassid stories,
and there are many others, but nothing to compare with Zen.
Zen has simply got the knack of hitting at the right thing
and indicating that which cannot be indicated.
And in such a simple way that you can miss it:
you will have to search for it, you will have to grope for it,
because the anecdote in itself is so simple
that you can miss it.
It is not very complex, in fact, the mind is not required;
rather, an opening of the heart, so that you can understand.

See...this small anecdote tells the whole significance of Zen:

Somebody asked the master, Bokuju:
We have to dress and eat every day—
how do we get out of all that?

Had he asked the same thing to Buddha,
the answer would not have been the same.
The answer would have come from the seed-mind.

The Significance of Zen

Buddha would have said: All is illusory—
eating, dressing, everything is illusory. Become more aware.
See the illusoriness and dreaminess of the world.
All is *maya*.
Become more aware and don't try to find how to get out of it,
because how can one get out of a dream?
One simply becomes aware and one is out.
Have you seen anybody ever getting out of a dream?
A dream is unreal, how can you get out of it?
The miracle is that you entered it in the first place—
because it is not there and you entered it!
And now you are creating more trouble for yourself
asking how to get out of it.
The same way as you entered it, get out of it!
How did you enter the dream? By believing that it was real.
That is the way one enters a dream—
by believing that it is real.
So simply drop the belief, and see that it is not real,
then you are out of the dream.
There are no steps to get out,
no techniques to get out, no methods.
Buddha would have said: Look...your whole life is a dream—
and you would have been out of it.

If the Chinese genius Confucius had been asked
—the balanced mind which is neither extrovert nor introvert—
he would have said: There is no need to get out of it.
Follow these rules and you will be able to enjoy it.
Confucius would have given a few rules:
those rules have to be followed, that's all.
One need not get out of it.
One simply has to plan his life in a right way.
One even has to plan the life of dream in a right way!
Confucius says that even if in your dream
you commit something wrong,
you have to ponder over it—
somewhere in your waking hours
you are not following the right path.
Otherwise how can you go wrong in the dream?
Settle something, balance something—
that's why he had three thousand, three hundred rules.

But in Japan there would have been a totally different answer:

with Buddha the answer would have come from the seed,
with Confucius from the tree—
from Bokuju it comes from the flower.
Of course these are different answers—
rooted in the same truth,
but not using the same symbols, they cannot.
What Bokuju says is simply flower-like,
it is the most perfect possibility.
Bokuju answered:
We dress, we eat.
Such a simple answer—and there is every possibility to miss.
You may think: What is he saying?
It looks like gibberish, nonsense. The man asked:
We have to dress and eat every day—
how do we get out of all that?
And Bokuju answered: We dress, we eat.

What is Bokuju saying, what is he indicating?
A very subtle indication. He is saying:
We also do it—we eat, we dress—but we eat so totally
that the eater doesn't exist, only eating.
We dress so totally that the dresser doesn't come into being,
but only dressing.
We walk, but there is no walker, just the walk.
So who is this asking to get out of it?

Look at the vast difference.
Buddha would have said that all this is a dream,
your eating, your dressing, your walking—
and Bokuju says that you are a dream.
Tremendous difference.
Bokuju is saying: Do not bring yourself in,
simply eat and walk and sleep.
Who is this asking to get out of it?
Drop this ego; it is non-existential,
and when you are not, how can you come out of it?
Not that walking is a dream, but the walker is the dream.
Not that eating is a dream, but the eater.

And watch minutely—
if you really are walking, is there any walker inside?
Walking happens, it is a process.
Legs move, hands move, you breathe more,
the wind blows in your face, you enjoy;

the faster you go, the more vitality you feel—
everything is beautiful. But is there really a walker?
Is there somebody sitting inside,
or does just the process exist?
If you become aware, you will find only the process exists.
The ego is illusory: it is just a mind-creation.
You eat, and you think there must be somebody who eats,
because logic says:
How can you walk without a walker inside?
How can you eat without an eater being there?
How can you love without a lover being inside?
This is what logic says. But if you have loved,
and if you have come to a moment where love really existed,
you must have known that there was no lover inside—
only love, a process, an energy. But nobody inside.

You meditate, but is there any meditator?
And when meditation comes to a flowering,
and all thoughts cease, who is there inside?
Is there somebody who says that all thoughts have ceased?
If that is there, then still the meditation has not flowered;
at least one thought is still there.
When meditation flowers
there is simply nobody to take note of it,
nobody to give it recognition,
nobody to say: Yes, it has happened.
The moment you say: Yes, it has happened—
it is lost already.

When there is really meditation, a silence pervades;
without any bounds a bliss throbs;
without any boundaries there is a harmony;
but there is nobody to take note.
There is nobody to say: Yes, this has happened.
That's why the Upanishads say that when a person says:
I have realised!
you can know well that he has not.
That's why all the Buddhas have said
that whenever somebody claims, the very claim
shows that he has not reached the final peak
because at the final peak the claimer disappears.
In fact, it has never been there.
Eating is not a dream—the eater is the dream.

The whole emphasis has changed from the seed to the flower.

That's why many people in the West think
that to call Zen, 'Zen Buddhism,' is not good,
because a vast difference is felt in the answers.
But they are wrong.
Zen Buddhism is absolute pure Buddhism,
even purified of Buddha, purified of Buddhist concepts.
It is the most essential, the purest *dhyan*,
the purest flowering of consciousness.
Without any centre, you exist.
Without there being anybody, you exist.
You are, and still you are not.
That's what Tilopa is emphasising:
no-self, *anatta*, emptiness, void.

What does Bokuju say? He says: We dress, we eat.
His answer is finished. His answer is complete, perfect.
He says simply: We eat, and we dress,
and we have never found any problem,
and we have never found anybody who can come out.
There is nobody inside.
Eating exists, dressing exists, ego does not.

He is saying: Don't ask a foolish question.
The questioner had said: I don't understand.
He may have come to find some rules and disciplines,
how to become a religious man,
how to drop these trivial things of eating and dressing,
that same routine;
every day, again and again, one goes on doing the same thing.
He must have been fed up, bored;
everybody comes to this point.
If you are a little intelligent,
you will have to come to a point when you will feel bored.
Only idiots and sages are never bored,
otherwise intelligent people are bound to get fed up.
What is going on?
Every day you go to sleep, just to get up again in the morning.
And then the breakfast, and then the going to the office,
and the this and the that.
And you know you are doing all this to go to sleep again,
and you know well that in the morning

The Significance of Zen

again the same routine will start.
One starts feeling robot-like.

And if you become aware,
as in India where people have become aware in the past,
that this has been going on for millions of lives,
you are bound to feel completely bored to death.
That's why they say: How to get out of it?
This wheel of life and death goes on,
grinding and grinding and grinding,
and, just like a broken gramophone record,
the same line goes on repeating.
This has happened to you millions of times.
You fell in love, you got married, you worked hard,
you gave birth to children, you struggled, you died.
Again, and again, and again,
and it goes on ad nauseam.
That's why, becoming aware of this phenomenon
of continuous rebirth, India became bored;
the whole consciousness became so fed up
that the whole effort became 'how to get out of it?'
That's what that man had come to ask Bokuju:
Help me to get out of it.
It is too much and I don't know from where to escape.
Getting dressed, and eating every day—
how to get out of this dead routine, this rut?
Says Bokuju: We dress, we eat.

He says many things.
He says that there is nobody to get out,
so, if there is nobody, how can you get bored?
Who will get bored?

I also get up every day in the morning, take my bath,
eat, dress, do everything that you do.
But I am not bored,
I can go on doing it until the very end of eternity.
Why am I not bored?
Because I am not there, so who is going to get bored?
And if you are not there,
who is going to say that it is a repetition?
Every morning is new, it is not a repetition of the past.
Every breakfast is new. Every moment is new and fresh

like the dewdrops on the grass in the morning.
It is because of your memory—collecting the past,
carrying the past, and always looking at the fresh moment
through the past, the dusty past—that you feel bored.

Bokuju lives in the moment
and doesn't bring in other moments to compare with it.
There is nobody who carries the past,
and there is nobody who thinks about the future.
There is only a life process, a river of consciousness,
which goes on moving from moment to moment,
always from the known into the unknown,
always from the familiar into the unfamiliar.
So who is there to be worried about getting out of it?
There is nobody.
Bokuju says: We eat and we dress, and it is finished!
We don't create a problem out of it.

The problem arises because of the psychological memory.
You always bring in your past. You always bring it in
to compare and to judge and to condemn.
If I show you a flower, you don't see it directly;
you say: Yes, this is a beautiful rose.
What is the need to call it a rose?
The moment you call it a rose, all the roses
that you have known in the past have come into it.
The moment you call it a rose,
you have compared it with other flowers,
you have identified it, you have categorised it.
The moment you call it a rose,
and the moment you call it beautiful,
all your concepts of beauty, memories of roses,
imaginations, everything, has come in.
The rose is lost in the crowd.
This rose is lost in the crowd.
This beautiful flower is lost
in your memories and imaginations and concepts
Then you will get fed up
because it will look like other roses.

What is the difference?
If you can look directly at this phenomenon, at this rose,
eyes fresh, empty of the past, consciousness clear,

perception unclouded, doors open, words non-existent,
if you can be here, now, with this flower for a little while,
then you will understand when Bokuju says:
We dress, we eat.

He is saying do everything so totally in the present
that you cannot feel it is a repetition.
And because you are not there, who is to carry the past,
and who is to imagine the future? Absent you exist,
and then a different quality of presence happens to you—
moment to moment new, flowing, loose, natural.
From one moment to another moment one simply slips,
just as a snake sometimes slips out of the old skin.
The old skin is left behind, he never looks back;
he doesn't try to carry the old skin.
A man of awareness simply slips from one moment to another,
just like a dewdrop slipping from the blade of grass,
not carrying anything.
A man of awareness has no cargo, he moves unburdened.
Then everything is new, and then no problems are created.

What Bokuju is saying is this:
It is better not to create a problem
because we have not known anybody to solve any problems, ever.
Once created, problems cannot be solved.
Don't create them, that is the only way to solve them.
Because once created, in the very creation
you have taken a false step. Now, whatsoever you do,
that false step won't allow you to solve it.
If you ask how to drop the ego
you have created a problem which cannot be solved.
Thousands of teachers exist who go on teaching you
how to solve it, how to be humble and how not to be an egoist.
Nothing happens—in your humility also, you remain egoists;
in your egolessness also, you carry a subtle ego.
No. Those who know will not help you to solve any problems.
They will simply ask where the ego is.
They will ask where, in fact, the problem is.
They will help you to understand the problem,
not to solve it, because the problem is false.
The answer cannot be right if the question is wrong.
If the very question is rooted in something wrong,
then all answers given will be futile

and they will lead you to more false questions.
It will become a vicious circle—
that's how philosophers become mad.
Not looking at the wrongness of the question
they create an answer;
and then the answer creates more questions.
No answer solves anything.

Then what is to be done? What does Zen say?
Zen says: Look at the problem itself,
there the answer is hidden.
Look at the question deeply,
and if the look is perfect, the question disappears.
No question is ever answered, it simply disappears;
and, when it disappears, it disappears without any trace.

He is saying:
Where is the problem? We also eat, we also dress,
but we simply eat and dress. Why create a problem?
Bokuju is saying: Accept life as it is.
Don't create problems.
One has to eat—eat.
There is hunger, you have not created it,
it has to be fulfilled—fulfill it.
But don't create a problem.

When people come to me this is the whole situation, every day.
They bring their problems
but I have not come across a single problem,
because there are none.
You create them, and then you want an answer to them.
There are people who will give you answers:
those are small teachings.
And there are people who will give you an insight
into your problem: that is the great teaching.
Small teachings lead to forced disciplines,
and great teachings allow you to become loose and natural.

Bokuju says: We dress, we eat.
But the man could not understand.
Of course, it is difficult to understand such a simple thing.
People can understand complex things
but they cannot understand simple things.

The Significance of Zen

Because a complex thing can be divided, analysed,
logically tackled, but what is to be done with a simple thing?
You cannot analyse it, you cannot cut it into pieces,
you cannot dissect it—there is nothing to dissect.
It is so simple. And because it so simple, you miss it.
The man could not understand.
But still, I think, the man was very sincere,
because he said: I don't understand.

There are very complex people who will nod their heads
to show that they have understood.
These are great fools: nobody can help them
because they go on pretending that they understand.
They cannot say that they don't understand.
If they say this, they will look idiotic to themselves.
They pretend. How can they not understand such a simple thing?
They go on showing that they have understood,
and now more complexities will arise.
In the first place there is no problem,
and in the second place they have understood the answer!
Problem doesn't exist, and now they have gained knowledge
about the problem: they say they understand!
They become more and more puzzled, just a mess inside.
Such people come to me and I can see inside them—
they are just a mess, a hotch-potch.
They have not understood anything.
They have not even understood what their problems are,
and they have the answers. Not only that,
they start helping others to solve their problems.

This man must have been sincere.
He said: I don't understand.
This is a good step towards understanding.
If you don't understand, you can understand;
the possibility is open.
You are humble, you recognise the difficulty,
you recognise that you are ignorant.
This is the first step towards knowing, towards understanding:
to recognise that you don't understand.
At least he understood this much.
And this is a great step.

Bokuju answered:

*If you don't understand,
put on your clothes and eat your food.*

Bokuju does not look very compassionate, but he is.
He is saying: You cannot understand,
because the mind never understands.
The mind is a great non-understander;
the mind is the very root of ignorance.
Why can't the mind understand?
Because the mind is just a tiny part of your being,
and the part cannot understand,
only the whole can understand.
Always remember this:
only your total being can understand something, no part can.
Neither your head nor your heart,
nor your hands, nor your legs, can understand—
only your total being.
Understanding is of the total,
misunderstanding is of the part.
The part always misunderstands,
because the part tries to pretend as the whole;
that is the whole problem.
The mind tries to say that it is the whole understanding,
but it is just a part.

When you fall asleep, where is your mind?
The body continues without it.
The body digests food; there is no need for the mind.
Your brain can be taken out completely
and your body will continue. It will digest food,
it will grow, it will throw dead things out of the body.
Now scientists have come to feel
that the mind is just a luxury.
The body has its own wisdom, it doesn't bother about the mind.
Have you ever observed
that the mind goes on playing at being the great knower,
without having the slightest feeling
that all that is important in the body goes on without it?
You eat food. The body doesn't ask the mind how to digest it;
and it is a very complex process.
It is not easy to transform food into blood,
but the body transforms it and goes on working.
It is a very complicated process

The Significance of Zen

because thousands of elements are involved.
In right proportions, the body releases juices,
which are needed to digest the food.
Then it absorbs that which is needed for the body
and it leaves that which is not needed,
it throws out the excreta.
In the body, every second, thousands of cells are dying;
the body goes on throwing them out of the bloodstream.
There are millions of needs for hormones, vitamins,
and millions of things,
and the body goes on finding them from the atmosphere.
When the body needs more oxygen, it takes deep breaths.
When the body doesn't need it, it relaxes breathing.
Everything goes on—
mind is just a part in this whole mechanism,
and not very essential.
Without the mind animals exist, trees exist,
and exist beautifully.
But the mind is a great pretender.
It simply pretends that it is the base, the foundation,
the peak, the climax. It goes on pretending.
You just watch your mind and you will see.
With this pretender you want to understand?
This is the only false note within you.

What is Bokuju saying? He says:
If you don't understand,
put on your clothes and eat your food.
Don't bother about understanding. You just be like us—
eat and dress, and don't try to understand.
The very effort, the very movement to understand
creates misunderstanding. There is no need.
Simply live and be.
That's what Bokuju says: Eat and dress, just be.
Forget about understanding, what is the need?
If trees can exist without understanding,
what is the need for you? If the whole existence
is there without understanding, why bother?
Why bring this small tiny mind in and create problems?
Relax and be!

Bokuju is saying that the understanding comes from the total.
You simply eat, don't try to understand.

You simply move, walk, love, sleep, eat, take your bath.
Be total. Let things happen. Simply be.
And don't try to understand, because the very effort to try,
the very effort to understand, creates a problem.
You become divided.
Don't create the problem—just be.

Try this sometime. I would like you to try this:
sometime go into the mountains for three weeks and just be.
Don't try to understand anything—just be, naturally loose.
When you feel like sleeping, go to sleep.
When you feel like eating, eat.
If you don't feel like eating, don't eat.
There is no urgency.
Just leave everything to the body, to the total.
Mind is a creator of problems.
Sometimes it says to fast when the body needs food.
Sometimes it says: Eat more, the food is very delicious!
And when the body says: Enough, wait,
don't force anything any more—
you don't listen to the total.
The total is wise.
In that total, your mind, your body, everything, is involved.

Not that I am saying cut the mind off—
that too would be unnatural, that too is a part.
The mind must have its own place, its own proportion,
but it should not be allowed to be the dictator.
If it becomes the dictator, then it creates problems.
And then it seeks solutions,
and solutions create more problems,
and you go on and on until you end up in a madhouse.

Mind's destiny is the madhouse.
Those who go fast, of course, reach earlier;
those who go slow, they reach a little later—
but everybody is in the queue.
Mind's destiny is the madhouse, because a part
trying to pretend to be the whole is already mad, insane.

And all religions have helped to create divisions in you.
All religions have helped the mind
to become more and more dictatorial.

The Significance of Zen

They say: Kill the body.
And you don't understand what you are doing,
and you start killing the body.
Mind and body and soul—they all exist together,
in a togetherness. They are a togetherness.
Don't divide; divisions are false, divisions are political.
If you divide, the mind becomes the dictator
because the mind is the most articulate part in the body.
There is nothing else in it.

It happens in life also:
if a man is more articulate, he will become a leader of men.
If he can talk well, if he is an orator,
if he can manipulate language, he will become the leader.
Not that he is capable of being a leader,
but he is a good talker, he impresses people's minds,
he is a good persuader, a good salesman, articulate.
That's why orators lead the world.
Of course, they lead it into a deeper and deeper mess
because they are not leaders of men.
They don't have any other quality than talk.
So your parliaments are nothing but talking-houses.
People go on talking, and the one
who can manipulate language better becomes the head.
That's why your parliaments and your madhouses
are not very different—they are the same.

The quality of being total is totally different.
It is not a question of being articulate,
it is rather a question of giving every part its proportion.
It is a harmony.
It is giving your life a harmonious rhythm
with everything existing in it.
Then the mind is also beautiful.
Then it doesn't lead you to the madhouses.
Then the mind becomes the greater mind,
the mind becomes the enlightenment.
But your whole exists as a whole;
you don't divide yourself; your wisdom remains undivided.
That's what Bokuju is saying,
and that is what Zen is all about.

That's why I say that Zen is a rare phenomenon.
No other religion has reached to such a great flowering.
Because Zen has come to understand
that the understanding is of the total—
you eat, you sleep, you be natural and you be total,
and don't try to divide yourself,
mind and body, soul and matter.
Don't divide. With division comes conflict and violence,
with division come millions of problems,
and then there are no solutions.
Rather, there is only one solution
and that is to be whole again,
to leave everything to the natural totality.

The mind will be there
but its function will be totally different.
I also use the mind. I am talking to you, the mind is needed.
For communication the mind is needed;
in fact it is a communication device.
For memory the mind is needed. It is a computer.
But to be, your whole is needed. In the body
—and when I say 'body' I mean your whole: body, mind, soul—
everything has its own functioning.
If I want to catch something, I will use my hand.
If I want to move, I will use my legs.
If I want to communicate, I will use my mind.
That's all. Otherwise I remain as a whole.
And when I use my hands, my whole backs my hands.
They are not used against the whole,
but with the co-operation of the whole.
When I use my legs and walk,
they are used by the whole, in co-operation.
In fact, they are functioning, walking for the whole,
not for themselves.
If I talk to you, communicate, I use the mind for the whole.
If I have something in my whole being
that I would like to communicate, I use my mind,
I use my hands and my gestures, I use my eyes;
but they are used by the whole.
The whole remains the supreme.
The whole remains the master.
When parts become the master, then you are falling apart,
then your togetherness will be lost.

Says Bokuju: If you don't understand, there is no need.
Don't be worried about it.
You just go and put on your clothes and eat your food.
I don't know what that man did, but to you I also say:
If you understand—beautiful.
If you don't understand—
go, put on your clothes and eat your food.
Because the understanding will come only as a shadow
of your total being.
Live life in its totality,
and don't be afraid of the total life.
Don't be a coward,
and don't try to escape to the mountains and the monasteries.

I have given you *sannyas* to live in the world
as totally as possible.
Just by living totally in the world you will transcend it.
Suddenly you will come to know
that you are in the world, but not of it.
I bring you a totally new concept of *sannyas*.
The old *sannyas* said: Escape, renounce!
But I tell you that those who escape are cowards.
And I tell you that those who escape are not total, not whole.
I tell you that those who escape are crippled.
It is not for you. You live life in its totality;
you live it, as wholly as possible.
And the more whole you are, the more holy you will become.
The quality of sacredness comes when one lives courageously
without fear, without hope, without desire.
One simply slips from one moment to another,
completely fresh and new.

This is what *sannyas* is to mean to you.
Sannyas is living life in its totality, moment to moment;
allowing it to happen without any conditions on your part.
And then, if you can allow this much,
life allows you a transcendence.
Remaining in the valley, you become the peak,
and only then it is beautiful.
If you go to the peak, the valley is lost—
and the valley has its own beauties.
If you remain in the valley, the peak is lost—
and the peak has its own beauties.

And I would like you to become a man of valley and peak, both together. Remaining in the valley, be a peak — and then you will be able to understand what Zen is.

Master and Disciple
22nd February 1975

Every time Lieh Tzu was not busy,
Yin Sheng took the opportunity to beg for secrets.
Lieh Tzu kept turning him away and would not tell him
until eventually he said:
I used to think you intelligent—
are you really as vulgar as all that?
Here, I will tell you what I learnt from my own master.

Three years after I began to serve the master,
my mind no longer dared to think of right and wrong,
and my mouth no longer dared to speak of benefit and harm.
It was only then
that I got so much as a glance from the master.

After five years
my mind was again thinking of right and wrong,
and my mouth was again speaking of benefit and harm.
For the first time the master's face relaxed into a smile.

After seven years I thought of whatever came into my mind
without any longer distinguishing between right and wrong,
and I said whatever came into my mouth
without any longer distinguishing between benefit and harm.
And for the first time
the master pulled me over to sit with him on the same mat.

After nine years
I thought without restraint of whatever came into my mind,
and said without restraint whatever came into my mouth
without knowing whether the right or wrong, benefit or harm,
were mine or another's,
and without knowing whether that master was my teacher or not.
Everything was the same.

Now you come to be my disciple,
and before even a year has gone round
you are indignant and resentful time and time again!

The greatest art in the world is to be a disciple.
It cannot be compared to anything.
It is unique and incomparable.
Nothing like it exists in any other relationship,
nothing like it can exist.

To be a disciple, to be with a master,
is to move into the unknown.
You cannot be very aggressive there. If you are aggressive,
the unknown will never be revealed to you.
It cannot be revealed to an aggressive mind.
The very nature of it is such
that you have to be receptive, not aggressive.

The search for truth is not an active search,
it is a deep passivity—
in your deep passivity you will receive.
But if you become too active and concerned, you will miss.
It is like being a womb, it is feminine,
you receive the truth as a woman receives a pregnancy.

Remember this...
then many things will become easier to understand.

To be near a master is to be just a passivity,
absorbing whatsoever the master gives
or whatsoever the master is—not asking.
The moment you start asking you have become aggressive,
the receptivity is lost, you have become active.
The passive, the feminine, is no longer there.
Nobody has ever reached the truth as a male—
aggressive, violent. That's not possible.
You reach very silently.
In fact, you wait and the truth reaches you.
The truth seeks you, like water seeks some hollow ground,
moves downwards, finds a place, and becomes a lake.

An active mind is too filled with itself;
an active mind thinks that it knows what truth is.
One has only to ask, at least the question is known;
only for the answer does one have to seek and search.
But when you become passive, even the question is not known.
How to ask? What to ask? For what to ask?
There is no question, one cannot do anything else but wait.
This is patience—and this is infinite patience—
because it is not a question of time, it is not a question
of you waiting for a few months, or a few years.
If you have patience for a few years, that won't help,
because a mind that thinks that it has to wait for three years
is not, in fact, waiting.
He is looking actively, to when the three years are over,
then he can jump, be aggressive, and ask;
then he can demand that the period of waiting be over,
that now he is entitled to know.
There is nothing like that.
Nobody is ever entitled to know the truth.

Suddenly the moment comes when you are ready,
and your patience has become not of time, but of eternity;
you are not waiting for something, but simply waiting,
because the waiting is so beautiful;
the waiting itself is such a prayerful mood,
the waiting itself is such a deep meditation,
the waiting itself is such a tremendous achievement—
who bothers about anything else?
When the waiting has become so total, so intense, so whole,
that time disappears
and the waiting takes the quality of eternity,
then immediately you are ready.
You are not entitled, remember—you cannot ask.
You are simply ready
and you are not even aware that you are ready.
Because the very awareness
will be a hindrance to your readiness;
the very awareness will show that the ego is there,
watching in the corner, hiding somewhere.

And the ego is always aggressive,
whether hiding or not hiding, apparent or not apparent.
Even hiding in the deepest corner of the unconscious,
the ego is aggressive. And when I say
that to become totally passive is the art of being a disciple,
I mean—dissolve the ego.
Then there is nobody who is asking, demanding,
then there is simply nobody—
you are a vacant house, a deep emptiness, simply waiting.
And suddenly, all that you could have asked for
is given to you, without you asking for it.

Jesus says: Ask, and it shall be given to you.
But that is not the highest teaching.
Jesus could not give the highest teaching
to the people who were around him
because they did not know how to be disciples.
In the Jewish tradition teachers have existed, and students,
but a disciple and a master is basically an Eastern phenomenon.
Teachers have existed—who have taught many things;
and students have existed, sincere students—
who have learnt much.

But Jesus couldn't find disciples there,
he couldn't give the highest teaching. He says:
Ask, and it shall be given to you.
Knock, and doors shall be opened unto you.
But I tell you, if you ask, you will miss;
if you knock, you will be rejected.
Because the very knocking is aggressive,
the very asking is of the ego.
In the very asking you are too much,
and the doors cannot be opened for you.

In the knocking, what are you doing? You are being violent.
No. At the doors of the temples knocking is not allowed.
You have to come to the doors so silently
that even the sound of your feet is not heard.
You come as a nothing, as if nobody has come.
You wait at the door
and whenever the door opens you will enter.
You are not in a hurry.
You can sit and relax at the door,
because the door knows better than you when to open,
and the master inside knows better than you
when it should be given.

Knocking at the door of the temple is vulgar;
asking the master is unmannerly—
because he is not going to teach you anything,
he is not a teacher.
He is going to toss something to you
from his innermost being—a treasure—
and unless you are ready, it cannot be done.
The pearls cannot be thrown before the swine.
The master has to wait until your swine has disappeared,
until you have awakened and you have become really human
and the animal is no longer there—
the aggressive, the vulgar, the violent.
The relationship between a master and a disciple
is not of a rape: it is of deepest love.

That is the difference between science and religion.
Science is like rape;
there is aggression towards nature to know its secrets.
Science is a violent effort to force nature

to reveal its secrets.
Religion is love, it is a persuasion, it is a silent waiting.
It is making oneself ready, prepared,
so that whenever the moment of your inner readiness comes,
suddenly there is a tuning, everything falls into line
and nature is revealed to you.
And this revelation is totally different.
Science may force nature to give a few facts—
but the truth? No.
Science will never be able to know the truth.
At the most, robbers, aggressive, violent people,
can snatch away a few facts. That's all.
And those facts will be of the surface.
The innermost centre will remain veiled for them
because to reach the innermost,
violence is not to be used—cannot be used.
The innermost centre must invite you,
only then can you enter there. Uninvited, there is no way.
As a guest, invited, you enter into the inner shrine.

The relationship between a master and a disciple
is the highest possibility of love—
because it is not a relationship of two bodies,
it is not a relationship of any pleasure, or any gratification,
it is not a relationship of two minds, two friends,
in subtle, psychic harmony. No.
It is neither bodily, nor sexual;
it is neither mental nor emotional.
It is two totals, coming together and merging into each other.

And how can you be a total if you ask a question?
If you are aggressive, you cannot be total.
A totality is always silent; there is no conflict within.
That's why you cannot be in conflict without.
Totality is serene and tranquil and collected.
It is a deep togetherness.
Waiting near a master, one learns how to be together,
with no movement. A simple unmoving centre simply waits;
thirsty of course, hungry of course,
feeling the thirst in every fibre of the body,
in every cell of the being—but waiting,
because the master knows better when the right moment comes.
Not knocking...

the temptation will be there,
and, when the master is available,
the temptation becomes very, very deep and intense.
Why not ask him? He can give, then why wait, why waste time?
No, it is not a question of wasting time.
Really, waiting patiently is the best use of time.
All else may be wasted but waiting is not,
because waiting is prayer, waiting is meditation,
waiting is all. Everything happens through it.

And I call it the greatest art. Why?
Because between a master and disciple
the greatest mystery is lived, the deepest is lived,
the highest flows.
It is a relationship between the known and the unknown,
between the finite and infinite,
between time and eternity,
between the seed and the flower,
between the actual and the potential,
between past and future.
A disciple is only the past; the master is only the future.
And here, this moment, in their deep love and waiting,
they meet.
The disciple is time, the master is eternity.
The disciple is mind and the master is no-mind.
The disciple is all that he knows,
and a master is all that cannot be known.
When the bridge happens between a master and a disciple,
it is a miracle. To bridge the known with the unknown,
and time with eternity, is a miracle.

Doing is on the part of the master,
because he knows what to do.
The doing is not on your part, should not be on your part,
because, by your very doing, you will disturb the whole thing.
You don't know what you are—how can you do anything?
A disciple waits, knowing well that he cannot do.
He does not know the direction,
he does not know what is good and what is bad,
he does not know himself. How can he do anything?
The doing is of the master;
but when I say that the doing is of the master,
don't misunderstand me.

Master and Disciple

A master never does anything—
if the disciple can wait,
the very being of the master becomes a doing.
Just his presence becomes a catalytic agent,
and many things start happening on their own accord.

When somebody asked the great master Zenerin:
What do you do with your disciples?
He said: What do I do? I don't do anything.
The questioner asked:
But so many things happen around you,
you must be doing something.
Zenerin said:
Sitting quietly, doing nothing,
spring comes, and the grass grows by itself.

This is what a master is doing:
sitting quietly, doing nothing,
waiting for the right moment, the spring.
Suddenly, when the disciple and the master meet,
there will be spring—
the spring comes, and the grass grows by itself.
And this is how it happens.
A master simply sits, not doing anything
and a disciple waits for the master to do something.
Then comes the spring.
And the moment they meet, the grass grows by itself.

In fact, truth is a happening; one has only to allow it.
Nothing is to be done directly; one has only to allow it.
You will not be able to know it, unless it happens,
because all you know is
that only when you do something does something happen.
When you don't do anything, nothing happens.
So you are completely oblivious
of a totally different dimension of things.
But, if you observe your own life,
you will see many things still happening without your doing.
What do you do when love happens?
The grass grows by itself.
Suddenly the spring is there and something flowers within you,
flowers for somebody—you are in love.
What have you done?

That's why people are so afraid of love—
because it is a happening, you cannot manipulate it,
you cannot be in control.
That's why people say that love is blind.
In fact, just the opposite is the case—
love is the only clarity of vision.
Love is the only eye, but people say that love is blind
because they cannot do anything about it.
It takes possession and they are no longer in control,
they are thrown off-centre. They say it is blind
because reason is not there—it is irrational.
It is like a madness; it is like a high fever;
it is something that has happened to you, like a disease.
It appears to be so, because you are no longer in control—
life has taken over.
Truth is of the quality of love.
That's why Jesus goes on saying, 'Love is God,' or 'God is love,'
because the quality is of the same source.
Truth also happens like love, you don't do anything about it.
You don't even knock on the door.

You breathe in, you breathe out; that is what life is.
How do you do it? Are you the doer?
Then hold your breath in, for a few seconds,
and you will come to know that you are not the doer.
You cannot hold it for long.
Within seconds the breath will force itself out.
Hold it out: within seconds you will find
you cannot do anything—
the breath is forcing itself in.
In fact, the grass grows by itself, just like breathing.
It grows of its own accord; you are not the doer.

But the ego avoids looking at such facts.
The ego looks only at things which you can do.
It chooses, accumulates things which can be done,
and it avoids, throws into the unconscious,
those things which happen. The ego is very choosey.
It doesn't look at life in its totality.

Truth is a happening, the final happening,
the ultimate happening, in which you dissolve into the whole
and the whole dissolves into you.

Master and Disciple

In the words of Tilopa, it is *mahamudra*,
the ultimate orgasm that happens
between one unit of consciousness and total consciousness,
the total ocean of consciousness—
between the drop and the ocean.
It is the total orgasm, in which both are lost into each other
and the identities dissolve.

The same happens between a master and a disciple.
The master is of the quality of the ocean
and the disciple is still a drop—
the finite meeting the infinite.
Much patience is needed,
infinite patience is needed. Hurry won't help.

Now, try to understand this beautiful Zen parable.
Each word has to be allowed to reach your deepest core of being,
because this is what you are here for.
If you can understand this story,
it will be easier for you to be closer and closer to me.

Every time Lieh Tzu was not busy,
Yin Sheng took the opportunity to beg for secrets.

Lieh Tzu was one of the masters of the school of Lao Tzu,
One of the enlightened disciples of Lao Tzu.
And Lieh Tzu was not an ordinary master,
not concerned with your small problems, your actions,
not concerned with small teachings.
Lieh Tzu was concerned only with the ultimate.
He had many disciples.

There are two types of disciples.
One type of disciple is chosen by the master;
another type of disciple is one who has chosen the master.
Their qualities differ.
This man, Yin Sheng, must have been one of the second category
—and vast is the difference.
When a master chooses you, it is totally different.
Of course, you will never be allowed to know
that the master has chosen you.
In fact, the master will persuade you in such a way
that you will feel that you have chosen him.

The Grass Grows By Itself

He has to be very subtle about it,
because if he allows you to know that he has chosen you,
your ego can create a disturbance,
because the ego likes to be the master;
the ego likes to be in control.
Every day I encounter the same situation:
I have not to allow you to know that I am choosing you,
I have to give you freedom to choose me.

But the difference is vast,
because when a master chooses a disciple,
he chooses with perfect understanding.
He looks through you, all your potentialities, possibilities,
past and future—the whole destiny is revealed to him.
But when you choose a master, almost always you will be wrong.
Because you grope in the dark.
Not knowing who you are, how can you choose?
Not knowing what truth is, how can you choose a master?
How can you judge?
Whatsoever you judge is going to be wrong.
I say unconditionally: it is not a question
of whether something can be wrong and something right.
No. Whatsoever you choose will be wrong,
because you are in darkness,
you don't have the inner light by which to judge.
You don't have any criterion, you don't have any touchstone.
You cannot know what is gold and what is not gold.
A sincere seeker simply allows the master to be;
a sincere seeker allows a master to choose him.
A foolish seeker tries to choose the master,
and then, from the very beginning, trouble arises

Lieh Tzu and his master, Lao Tzu,
had a totally different quality of relationship.
Lao Tzu had chosen Lieh Tzu.
This Yin Sheng had chosen Lieh Tzu,
and when a disciple chooses he is aggressive—
because of the very choice the aggression starts.
And a master cannot reject you, even if you choose him,
just out of his compassion he cannot reject you.

Every time Lieh Tzu was not busy,
Yin Sheng took the opportunity to beg for secrets.

That begging is not really begging,
it is just a way to snatch.
In fact, he is aggressive, not a beggar,
the begging is just diplomatic. He is a thief, not a beggar.
Whenever he found any opportunity and Lieh Tzu was not busy,
he started begging for the secrets.
Lieh Tzu kept turning him away and would not tell him
until eventually he said....
Many times Lieh Tzu avoided, postponed, and said:
Sometime I will tell you, some other time,
it is not the right moment. You are not ripe.
But Yin Sheng persisted
until eventually Lieh Tzu had to say the truth. He said:
I used to think you intelligent—
are you really as vulgar as all that?

What is the vulgarity?
Secrets cannot be asked for, you have to earn them.
You have to become capable.
Secrets are gifts from the master: you cannot steal them,
you cannot beg them, you cannot snatch them,
you cannot rob them—there is no way.
Secrets can only be gifts, nothing else.
So you have to be capable,
capable so that the master can give them to you as gifts.
He would like to share them,
but you have to rise above your ordinary mind,
because the ordinary mind will not be able to share.
That's what Jesus goes on saying:
Pearls cannot be thrown before the swine.
Because the swine won't understand,
the understanding is not there.
You can understand words: those secrets are not words.
You can understand concepts: those secrets are not concepts.
They are not philosophies, doctrines.
Those secrets are the innermost energy of the master,
his treasure of being. If you rise higher and higher,
then only will you be nearer and nearer the master,
and only when the master feels that you can sit on the same mat
can the secrets be given to you. Not before.
Even if he wants to give, he cannot. To whom?
He would like to give them out of his compassion,
but they will be simply wasted.

It happened in the same way that
a Sufi mystic, Dhun-nun had a disciple.
The disciple must have been like Yin Sheng,
persistent, asking again and again.
One day, Dhun-nun gave him a stone
and told him to go to the market, to the vegetable market,
and to try to sell it.
The stone was very big, it looked beautiful.
But the master said: Don't sell it, just try to sell it:
observe, go to many people and just report to me
how much we can get for it from the vegetable market.
The man went. Many people looked at it and they thought:
It can be a good show-piece, our children can play with it,
or we can use it as measures for our vegetables.
So they offered, but just few small coins, like ten paise.
The man came back. He said:
At the most, we can only get ten paise for it—
and responses were different, from two paise to ten.

The master said: Now you go to the gold market
and ask people there. But don't sell it, just enquire how much.
From the gold market the disciple came, very happy,
and he said: These people are wonderful.
They are ready to give a thousand rupees for this.
Responses were different,
from five hundred to a thousand rupees.

The master said: Now you go to the jewellers, but don't sell it.
He went to the jewellers. He couldn't believe it.
They were ready to offer fifty thousand rupees.
And when he wouldn't sell, they went on increasing the offers—
they reached one hundred thousand rupees.
But the man said: I am not going to sell it.
They said: We offer two hundred thousand rupees,
three hundred thousand rupees, or whatsoever you say.
But sell it!
The man said: I cannot sell. I am just to enquire.
He couldn't believe it—these people were mad.
He himself thought that the price that was offered
in the vegetable market was enough.

He came back. The master took the stone and said:
We are not going to sell it,
but now you know that it depends on you,

Master and Disciple

on if you have the touchstone, the understanding.
You go on asking questions
and you live in the vegetable market.
You live in the vegetable market
and you have the understanding of that market.
Then you ask for valuable secrets: you ask for diamonds.
First become a jeweller, and then come to me.
Then I will teach you.

A certain quality of understanding is needed,
only then can certain truths be given to you.
And secrets? You cannot ask for them,
because in the very asking
you show that you come from the vegetable market.
You have to wait; you have to wait infinitely.
Then you show that you are ready to sacrifice
your whole life for them.
Then you show how much you value the secrets—
you are ready to sacrifice yourself completely.
Then the master simply shares his being with you.
Nothing is to be given, because these are not things.
Energy simply jumps from the master towards you like a flame.
It enters you and transfigures you completely.

*I used to think you intelligent—
are you really as vulgar as all that?*
This persistent asking shows a vulgar mind.
You don't understand what you are asking.
Juvenile, childish, you seem to be absolutely uncultured,
not knowing with whom you are, not knowing what you are asking.

And then he told his own story with his own master.
It is a rare story.

Here, I will tell you what I learnt from my own master.

His own master was Lao Tzu, the source of the Taoist tradition,
one of the greatest beings who has ever walked on the earth.
Says Lieh Tzu:
*Three years after I began to serve the master,
my mind no longer dared to think of right or wrong,
and my mouth no longer dared to speak of benefit and harm.
It was only then*

that I got so much as a glance from the master.
Three years passed. He simply served the master.
What else can you do? You can simply serve the master.
Nothing else can be done by a disciple.
No questioning. No asking. No demanding.
A disciple simply becomes a shadow of the master, serves him,
and through service, through his love, reverence, trust,
a change starts in the mind.
Says Lieh Tzu:
...my mind no longer dared to think of right and wrong.
It became almost impossible
to think about what is right and what is wrong.
When you live near a master, you need not think.
You simply move with him. You simply follow his movements.
You leave everything to him. You surrender.

Says Lieh Tzu:
*My mind no longer dared to think...
and my mouth no longer dared to speak of benefit and harm.*
Because in living near a master
your whole attitude starts changing. For the first time,
from the window of the master, you look at the total:
where wrong and right meet and mingle with each other,
where darkness and light are no more separate.
Says Heraclitus:
God is night and day,
summer and winter,
hunger and satiety.
Through the master first glimpses start coming to you.
The master becomes a window: the closer you come
the more your own understanding is thrown into chaos.
Whatever you knew before becomes absolutely useless, futile.
You are shaken. Your whole foundation is shaken.
You are thrown off-gear.
You no longer know what is right and what is wrong.
You have looked through the master at the whole,
and the total comprehends all.
The total comprehends all contradictions,
the total comprehends all paradoxes,
in the total all opposites meet and become one.
That's why Lieh Tzu said that he no longer dared to think
of what was wrong and what was right.

All the criteria of right and wrong dropped.
All the concepts of what is benefit and what is harm
simply evaporated.
*It was only then
that I got so much as a glance from the master.*

Three years of deep trust, service, and when the master saw
that now the old mind was no longer functioning
—the old mind, which lived in opposites, in divisions,
good and evil, ugly and beautiful, this and that—
that dividing mind was no more,
*it was only then
that I got so much as a glance from the master.*

What does Lieh Tzu mean?
Is it that for three years the master never looked at Lieh Tzu?
That is impossible. Serving the master continuously,
the master must have looked millions of times.
Then what does he mean by a glance?

A look and a glance are totally different.
A look is a passive thing.
When I look at you, my eyes function as a window,
you are mirrored, it is not a glance.
A glance means that my eyes don't function as windows,
but that my eyes start functioning
as a pouring of my energy into you.
They are not passive; they are loaded with the master's energy.
When the look is loaded with the master's innermost energy,
then it becomes a glance. It is a very creative force.
It simply goes to your very heart, like an arrow,
it penetrates to your very deepest core.
In a sense it is like an arrow, because it penetrates;
in another sense it is like a seed—you become pregnant.
A glance is a look
that makes you pregnant with the energy of the master.
A glance is totally different from a look. In a glance
the master travels from his own being to your centre.
A glance is a bridge. The master
must have looked at Lieh Tzu many times in three years,
but it was not a glance.
And you will know the difference
only when I give you a glance. Sometimes, I give you a glance—

but whenever I give the glance to a certain person,
only he knows, nobody else can know it.
The glance has to be earned, you have to be ready for it.
The look is okay,
but the glance has a very intense energy in it.
It is a transfer of the master's being,
his first effort to penetrate you.
*It was only then
that I got so much as a glance from the master.*
Remember the difference between a look and a glance.
A look is just a look—nothing more.
A glance is qualitatively different—something moves.
The look becomes the vehicle—
it is no longer empty, something travels with it.

If you have fallen in love with somebody you may know
what a glance is. The same woman had looked at you many times,
but it was an ordinary look—as everybody else looks at you.
Then suddenly one day, a spring morning,
she gives you a glance.
It is totally different; it is an invitation;
it is an offer; it is a call.
Suddenly something pierces your heart.
Now the woman is no longer the same,
and you also are no longer the same.
Something has happened between you.
Something only you two will know, something absolutely private.
It is not public, nobody else will be aware
that something has happened: that a look has become a glance.

But this is nothing, a love glance is nothing
compared to when a master looks at you,
and it is no longer a look but a glance.
Because when two lovers look at each other
with a loving glance, they stand on the same plane.
The glance cannot be very loaded,
it is just like a river moving on the same plane.
When a master looks at you, it is like a tremendous waterfall,
because the planes are different.
It is as if Niagara is falling into you.
You are completely washed away
and you will never be the same again.
You cannot be the same again—there is no return.

Master and Disciple

Once a master has glanced at you, your innermost being
hums in a different way, lives in a different rhythm.
In fact you are no longer the same:
the old has disappeared through the glance
and a new being has come into being.
That's what Lieh Tzu says—
for three years of serving the master continuously,
waiting and waiting, not asking anything,
one day, he got a glance from the master.

After five years
my mind was again thinking of right and wrong,
and my mouth was again speaking of benefit and harm.
For the first time the master's face relaxed into a smile.

Try to penetrate this story: this is your story.
It is not something that happened in the past,
it is something which is going to happen in the future.
All Zen stories are future stories about you.
So don't think it is something that happened in the past.
Zen is never in the past, it is always in the future.
And you have to bring it into the present.
What happened? After three years of serving the master
he didn't dare to think of what was right and wrong,
didn't dare to say what was right and wrong,
what was harmful and what was beneficial.
Then what happened after the glance?
... my mind was again thinking of right and wrong,
and my mouth was again speaking of benefit and harm.
What happened?

First you think something is right and something is wrong,
because society has conditioned you that way.
It is not your thinking, it is not you,
it is the society in you. Society has conditioned your mind.
It has penetrated within you and controls you from there.

Now scientists say that sooner or later we will be able
to fix electrodes in the deepest part of the mind and,
through those electrodes, a man will be able to be controlled.
The government will be able to control the whole country,
and you will not know that somebody else is controlling you.
You will feel that you are doing these things.
You can be pacified immediately: a knob has only to be pushed.

You can be made angry: a knob has only to be pushed.

Delgado did a very famous experimen
He fixed an electrode, a small, tiny electrode,
in the brain of a bull. Then he gave a public demonstration.
He had a small mechanism in his hand, just a small radio
with a few buttons on it. He pushed one button
and the bull rushed towards him, ferocious,
and everybody became concerned that Delgado would be killed.
Just in the nick of time, exactly when the bull
was going to penetrate Delgado, he pushed another button.
Suddenly, the bull stopped as if dead, like a statue.
The inside electrode was controlled by the wireless—
the bull would become ferocious just by pushing a button,
and it could be stopped just by pushing a button.

This is a very, very new finding
but society has been doing it since prehistorical days
in a different way, in a subtle way.
Society doesn't fix an electrode in your mind
although soon it will do that,
because it will be cheaper, and easier,
and then there will be no possibility for human freedom.
Delgado has done one of the most dangerous things,
more dangerous than atomic energy, an atom bomb, or an H-bomb—
because they can kill your bodies,
but Delgado can kill your very soul,
the very possibility of your freedom.
And you will not be able to know
that you are functioning because of somebody else's directions,
you will think that you are doing it.

The same is being done by society
in a very subtle, primitive way.
Society teaches you what is right and what is wrong.
From the very childhood it forces
what is right and what is wrong onto your mind
and then continuous repetition hypnotises you—
the continuous repetition and feedback.
Whenever you do right you are appreciated,
and whenever you do wrong you are condemned.
Whenever you do right, there is a positive feedback;
prizes are given to you, appreciations.

Whenever there is something wrong,
a negative feedback is given; you are punished, condemned.
This is how society has been fixing the electrode inside you.
Then it controls. If your society has conditioned you
to be a vegetarian, you cannot eat meat.
Not that meat cannot be eaten,
but simply the electrode, the conditioning, controls
and, seeing the meat, you will start vomiting.
It is nothing that you are doing, it is being done
by society, and every society conditions in its own way.
That's why it is very difficult to live in another society;
to live in a foreign country becomes difficult.
Your conditionings are different
and their conditionings are different
and all moralities are nothing but conditionings.
So when a person starts moving
towards ultimate freedom and truth,
first the conditioning of the society falls.

That's what happened to Lieh Tzu.
After three years of serving the master, watching, living,
being with him, he came to know that all right and wrong
are just social conditionings. They fell.
Then arises your own conscience. The real conscience.
The conscience that you carry right now is false,
it is borrowed.
Then arises your own conscience: then you have
your own vision of what is right and what is wrong.
That is what happened.

After five years
my mind was again thinking of right and wrong,
and my mouth was again speaking of benefit and harm.
For the first time the master's face relaxed into a smile.

Not that the master was continuously sad
for these eight years.
Hard, serious? No! A master like Lao Tzu is always laughing.
He is not a serious man. Seriousness is a disease.
An enlightened man is always playful,
his whole life is nothing but a play. How can he be serious?

What happened?
For these eight years, did Lao Tzu never laugh nor smile?

No, that is not the point: he must have laughed many times,
and he must have smiled many times.
But for Lieh Tzu, in his innermost being,
something happened on that day:
for the first time the master's face relaxed into a smile.
A master has to haunt the disciple continuously;
he has to be very hard;
out of compassion, he has to work continuously.
This is about the inner face, not about the outer face.
For these eight years Lao Tzu must have followed
the innermost being of Lieh Tzu with a very hard face,
very hard, for the inner discipline.
Then seeing that Lieh Tzu's own conscience had evolved,
he must have smiled, for the first time.
That smile was concerned with the inner, not the outer face.
For the first time, Lieh Tzu felt many smiles
from the master falling on him like showers.
He could feel that the master had relaxed about him—
no longer hard, no longer a taskmaster. He had smiled.

Once your own conscience has arisen,
there is no need for the master to be hard on you.
He had to be hard because you had a false conscience
in the first place. That had to be destroyed.
Then he had to be hard
because your own conscience had to be crystallised.
When it has crystallised, you have your own centre of being;
then the master can smile and relax. Half the work is done.
Now there is no need for any outer discipline
from the master for you. You have your own conscience.
Now you have your own inner light,
which will show you what is wrong and what is right.
Now you can move on your own.

That is the meaning of the master smiling—it is felt.
When really you attain to your own conscience, you will feel
the master's smiles falling within you, showering;
they will surround you from every corner of your being.
That is why the master celebrates
the birth of your inner conscience.

After seven years I thought of whatever came into my mind

*without any longer distinguishing between right and wrong,
and I said whatever came into my mouth
without any longer distinguishing between benefit and harm.
And for the first time
the master pulled me over to sit with him on the same mat.*

Again, it is like a spiral or like a mountain path.
You come again to the same point at a higher altitude,
again and again, the inner spiral.
The false conscience fell, the conditioning of society fell,
your own inner conscience arose. Now that too disappears.

*After seven years I thought of whatever came into my mind
without any longer distinguishing between right and wrong,
and I said whatever came into my mouth
without any longer distinguishing between benefit and harm.*

This is total relaxation.
A conscience, an inner conscience, is also needed
because you are not absolutely natural.
An outer conscience is needed
because you don't have an inner conscience.
The inner conscience is needed
because you are not absolutely natural yet:
something wrong can happen through you.
But when you are absolutely natural,
what Tilopa calls 'loose and natural',
then no harm can happen through you.
You simply are no more; you cannot harm.
Now there is no need, so your inner conscience also dissolves.
Now you become like a small child, simple and pure,
saying things that happen to you,
thinking things that happen to you.
Thoughts float in your mind, but you are not concerned;
your mouth says things, you are not concerned.
It is like a small child, or like a madman: absolutely relaxed,
as if there is nobody in control.
And when the control is completely lost, the ego disappears
because the ego is nothing but the controller—
when there is no control, who are you?
You are just like a river flowing towards the ocean,
or like a cloud floating in the sky.
You are no longer there; the human, the ego, has disappeared.

Now you are simply natural.

After seven years I thought of whatever came into my mind...
You cannot do anything, because there is nobody to do.
If thoughts come, they come.
If they don't come, okay; if they come, okay.
The mouth says something—there is nobody to control it,
so it says. Sometimes it doesn't say anything.
Sometimes somebody asks and no answer comes;
such a man will remain silent.
Sometimes there is nobody asking anything
and this man laughs and answers, because it comes.
This man behaves like a madman!

In India, there is a sect, a particular sect, called *baul*—
the word *baul* means the mad.
They live in this third state continuously.
They do whatsoever happens: no good, no bad,
no choice on their part.
They move like winds,
and they are one of the most beautiful phenomena in the world.
They dance, they sing, even sometimes when there is nobody,
on a lonely path, they will still be singing;
like a flower that has come to bloom on a lonely path
where nobody walks.
But the flower has the fragrance to spread,
and it goes on spreading the fragrance.
They live simply 'loose and natural'.

And for the first time
the master pulled me over to sit with him on the same mat.

Now the disciple has disappeared; the ego is no longer there.
Now the master and the disciple have become one,
now there is no distinction. The master pulled Lieh Tzu over,
for the first time
pulled him over to sit with him on the same mat.
Just symbolic. But, deep inside, very, very significant.
The master has pulled him towards him now,
seeing that no barrier exists, there is no ego to resist.
When the disciple disappears, the master also disappears.

The master was not there, in fact, from the very beginning.
It was only because of the ego of the disciple

that he was the master.
The disciple was ignorant, that's why he was the master.
Now there is no disciple and no master. Both have disappeared.

The master has pulled him onto his own mat;
inside, the master has pulled him and they have become one.
This is *mahamudra*.
This is the orgasm
that happens between a master and a disciple when they meet.
A faint glimpse can come to you
through sexual orgasm, very faint, very pale.
But it is difficult to have any other parallel,
that's why I say through sexual orgasm—
something of the same happens. Something.
As a drop can be compared to the ocean—just like that.
Sexual orgasm is like a drop,
and when a spiritual orgasm happens between a master
and a disciple it is an oceanic feeling.

*After nine years
I thought without restraint of whatever came into my mind,
and said without restraint whatever came into my mouth
without knowing whether the right or wrong, benefit or harm
were mine or another's,
and without knowing whether that master was my teacher or not.
Everything was the same.*

First the good and bad disappeared,
then benefit and harm disappeared, and then the idea:
Who is who?
You and me, I and thou, they disappeared.

Martin Buber has written a beautiful book, 'I and Thou'.
Jewish mysticism comes to this point
then remains stuck there. It is one of the very high points,
where the disciple and the master are the seeker and the whole.
They come to a point of direct dialogue between 'I' and 'Thou',
but they remain there.
Eastern mysticism takes the final jump—
'I' and 'Thou' also disappears.
The dialogue disappears. There is only silence.
Everything was the same.
Now Lieh Tzu was not even aware whether Lao Tzu was his master

or not. He was not aware whether he was a disciple or not.

In such moments many unbelievable things have happened
in the history of Zen.
The master always hits the disciple many times in many years.
Sometimes he throws him out of the door and kicks him!
Zen masters are very harsh.
And then the disciple becomes enlightened,
after twenty or thirty years of hard work and discipline
with the Master. And he comes and he slaps the master—
this has never happened anywhere before.
And the master laughs, a belly-laugh, and he says:
Exactly right. You did well.

It happened once that a disciple was going on a journey
and the master called him and hit him hard on the head
and slapped him. And the disciple said:
This is too much. I have not done anything.
I have not even uttered a single word.
I entered your room and you started hitting me.
This is too much.
The master said: No!
You are going on a journey and I can see
that the moment you come back, you will be enlightened.
And this is my last chance to hit you!

Now you come to be my disciple—said Lieh Tzu to Yin Sheng—
*and before even a year has gone round
you are indignant and resentful time and time again.*

It took twenty-four years for Lieh Tzu to come to a point
where the master pulled him onto his mat,
and opened his heart and the hidden-most secret of his being.
And this disciple had only been here for one year
and he felt resentful, aggressive, angry,
because Lieh Tzu wouldn't answer his questions
and wouldn't give him the secrets he was hankering for.

What is one year in the infinite expanse of eternity?
Nothing. But your hurry makes it look very, very long.
Twenty-five centuries have passed since Lieh Tzu was.
If he came back, he would not be able to believe
that it has become almost impossible for people

Master and Disciple

to wait for even one year.
I have come across people who say:
We have come only for three days.
I have come across people who meditate once,
and then they come to me and they say:
Nothing has happened yet.

Man has become more and more stupid, vulgar.
You can get small things easily,
they are like seasonal flowers: you put the seed in the soil,
and within three weeks they sprout.
But, by the season's end, they will be gone.
They are momentary.
You can have instant coffee:
you cannot have instant meditation.
In the mind of the West particularly,
time is too important, too heavy. The West is time obsessed.
Listening to these Eastern tales, you may enjoy them,
but you must be aware about your own time obsession.
In the West everything is done in such a hurry
that you cannot enjoy anything.
You move from one place to another, always on the go,
travelling fast. The faster you go,
the less significance there is in travelling,
because you go from one point to another
and all that is in between is lost.
To travel by a bullock-cart has a beauty of its own.
To travel by a jet plane is foolish
because it is not travel at all. It may be a business trip.
That's okay. For business it's okay. You save time.
But for travelling, for travelling you have to move slowly.
There is nothing like wandering on your feet,
then you enjoy each moment of it—each tree that passes by.
You become one with millions of things,
and you are enriched through it.

Because of time obsession, speed has become the only goal.
You don't know where you are going,
but you are very happy because you are going fast.
The direction is lost but speed is in your hand.

This mind will not be able to seek the ultimate,
because the ultimate means the eternal.

The Grass Grows By Itself

It is not like a seasonal flower:
it is the ultimate, eternal tree.
For it to become a soil, and for it to take roots in you,
infinite patience and waiting is needed.
If you can only wait,
then all else, I can promise, will come.
You simply wait with me, and everything will follow.
But don't be in a hurry and don't ask for secrets—
they will be given to you when you are ready.
They are always given.
In fact, to say that they are given is not exactly right.
When you are ready,
suddenly you will find that they were always with you.
When you are ready, you will suddenly find
that whatsoever you were trying to achieve
was already within you.
You had it always: it was already the case.
The master is just a catalytic agent;
he sits, silently, quietly, not doing anything.
Spring comes and the grass grows by itself.

Emptiness and the Monk's Nose
23rd February 1975

Sekkyo said to one of his monks:
Can you get hold of emptiness?

I'll try, said the monk,
and he cupped his hands in the air.

That's not very good, said Sekkyo,
You haven't got anything there.

Well, master, said the monk,
please show me a better way.

Thereupon, Sekkyo seized the monk's nose
and gave it a great yank.

Ouch! yelled the monk. You hurt me!

That's the way to get hold of emptiness,
said Sekkyo.

Man is too full of himself
and that is his undoing.

Man should be like a hollow bamboo,
so that existence can pass through him.
Man should be like a porous sponge—not hard—
so that the doors and the windows of his being are open,
and existence can pass from one end to another
without any hindrance; in fact, finding no one inside.
The winds blow—they come in from one window
and they go out from another window of his being.
Nobody is found within.
This emptiness is the highest bliss possible.

But you are like a hard, unporous rock,
or like a hard steel rod. Nothing passes through you.
You resist everything. You don't allow.
You go on fighting on all sides and in all directions
as if you are in a great war with existence.

There is no war going on, you are simply befooled by yourself.

Nobody is there to destroy you. The whole supports you;
the whole is the very earth on which you are standing,
the very sky in which you breathe, you live.
In fact, you are not—only the whole is.

When one understands this, by and by one drops
the inner hardness, there is no need for it.
There is no enmity, the whole is friendly towards you.
The whole cherishes you, loves you.
Otherwise, why are you here?
The whole brings you forth,
like a tree is brought forth by the earth.
The whole would like to participate in all your blessings,
in all the celebrations that are possible.
When you flower, the whole will flower through you;
when you sing, the whole will sing through you;
when you dance, the whole will dance with you.
You are not separate.

The feeling of separateness creates fear,
and fear makes you unporous.
The feeling of insecurity,
as if the whole is going to destroy you,
the feeling that you are a stranger here, an outsider,
and that you have to fight your way inch by inch
towards your destiny, makes you a hard steel rod.
Of course, then many things simply disappear from your life.
You live in anguish, you live in anxiety,
you live in intense pain, but you live this of your own accord.
Be porous. Be floating. Fight is not needed at all.
Rather, a merger is needed.

These are the two attitudes open to man:
the attitude of a warrior and the attitude of a lover.
It is your choice—you can choose.

But remember...certain consequences will follow.

Emptiness and the Monk's Nose

If you choose the path of the warrior
and you become a fighter with everything that surrounds you,
you will always be in misery.
This is creating a hell around you;
in the very attitude of fighting the hell is created.
Or you can become a lover, a participant,
then this whole is your home; you are not a stranger.
You are at home. There is no fight.
You simply flow with the river.
Then, ecstasy will by yours;
then each moment will become ecstatic, a flowering.

There is no hell except you
and there is no heaven except you.
It is your attitude, how you look at the whole.
Religion is the way of the lover:
science is the way of the fighter.

Science is the way of the will, as if you are here to conquer,
to conquer nature, to conquer nature's secrets;
as if you are here to enforce your will and domination
on existence. This is not only foolish, it is futile also.
Foolish because it will create a hell around you,
and futile because finally you will become
more and more dead, less and less alive;
you will lose all possibilities of being blissful.
And, in the end, you will have to come back from it,
because you can go for a while on the path of the will,
but only frustration and more frustration will happen
through it. You will be defeated more and more.
You will feel more and more impotent,
and more and more enmity will be around you.
You will have to come back from it—grudgingly, resistant,
but you will have to come back from it.
Finally, nobody can rest with a fighting attitude,
because with a fighting attitude no rest is possible,
you cannot relax.

The path of religion is the path of love.
From the very beginning you are not fighting anybody.
The whole exists for you, and you exist for the whole,
and there is an inner harmony.
Nobody is here to conquer anybody else. It is not possible.

Because how can one part conquer another part?
And how can a part conquer the whole?
These are absurd notions
which only create nightmares for you, nothing else.
See the whole situation...
you come out of the whole and you dissolve into it,
and, in between, you are every moment part of it.
You breathe it, you live it,
and it breathes through you, it lives through you.
Your life and its life are not two things—
you are just like a wave in the ocean.

Once you understand this, meditation becomes possible.
Once you understand this, you relax.
You throw off all the armour that you have created around you
as a security. You are no longer afraid.
Fear disappears and love arises.
In this state of love, emptiness happens.
Or, if you can allow emptiness to happen,
love will flower in it.
Love is a flower of emptiness, total emptiness—
emptiness is the situation.
It can work both ways.

So there are two types of religion.
One which creates emptiness in you and around you
so that a flowering becomes possible;
you have created the situation,
now the flower bubbles up automatically.
Finding no resistance, the seed suddenly blooms into a flower.
There is a jump in your being, an explosion.
Buddhism and Zen follow this path—
they create emptiness in and around you.

There is another path also, a second type of religion,
which creates love in you, which creates devotion in you.
Meera and Chaitanya love, and they love the total so deeply
that they find their beloved everywhere;
on every leaf, on every stone, is the signature of the beloved.
He is everywhere.
They dance because there is nothing else to do but celebrate.
And everything is ready—
only the celebration has to start on your part.

Emptiness and the Monk's Nose

Nothing else is lacking.
A *bhakta,* a lover, simply celebrates, enjoys.
And in that enjoyment of love and celebration,
the ego disappears and emptiness follows.

Either you create emptiness,
like a Buddha, Tilopa, Sekkyo, and others;
or you create love, like Meera, Chaitanya, Jesus.
Create one and the other follows,
because they cannot live separately,
they don't have any separate existence.
Love is one face of emptiness;
emptiness is nothing but love in another aspect,
they come together. If you bring one, you invite one,
the other follows automatically as a shadow of it.
It depends on you.
If you want to follow the path of meditation, become empty.
Don't bother about love—it will come of its own accord.
Or, if you find it very difficult to meditate, then love,
then become a lover,
and meditations and emptinesses will follow you.

This is how it should be because
there are two types of human mind: the feminine and the male.
The feminine mind can love easily but to be empty is difficult.
And when I say feminine mind, I don't mean females,
because many females have male minds,
and many males have feminine minds.
So they are not equivalent.
When I say feminine mind, I don't mean the feminine body—
you may have a feminine body but not a feminine mind.
The feminine mind is the mind that feels love easier,
that's all. That is my definition of the feminine mind:
it is one who feels love easily, naturally,
who can flow into love without any effort.
The male mind is one for whom love is an effort—
he can love but he will have to do it.
Love cannot be his whole being—it is just one thing
of many other things, not even the most important.
He can sacrifice his love for science,
he can sacrifice his love for the country,
he can sacrifice his love for any trivial affair,
for business, for money, for politics.

Love is not such a deep thing with him, a male mind.
It is not as effortless as it is for a feminine mind.
Meditation is easier. He can become empty easily.

So this is my definition:
if you find being empty easy, then do that.
If you find it is very difficult,
then don't be unhappy and don't feel hopeless.
You will always find love easier.
I have not come across a man who finds both difficult.
So, there is hope for everybody.
If meditation is difficult, love will be easier, it has to be.
If love is easier, meditation will be difficult.
If love is difficult, meditation will be easier.
So just feel yourself.

And this is not concerned with your body,
not with your physical structure, your hormones. No.
It is a quality of your inner being.
Once you find it, things become very, very easy,
because then you won't try on the wrong path.
You can try on the wrong path for many lives
but you will not attain anything.
And if you try on the right path,
even the first step can become the last,
because you simply, naturally flow into it.
Nothing like effort exists—effortlessly you flow.

Zen is for the male mind.
Soon I will balance it by talking about Sufism,
because Sufism is for the feminine mind.
These are the two extremes—Zen and Sufism.

Sufis are lovers, great lovers.
In fact, in the whole history of human consciousness,
more daring lovers than Sufis have never existed,
because they are the only ones
who have turned God into their beloved.
The God is the woman and they are the lovers.
Soon I will balance.

Zen insists on emptiness,
that's why in Buddhism there is no concept of God,

it is not needed. People in the West cannot understand
how a religion exists without the concept of a God.
Buddhism has no concept of any God—there is no need,
because Buddhism insists on simply being empty,
then everything follows. But who bothers?
Once you are empty, things will take their own course.
A religion exists without God. This is simply a miracle.
In the West, people who write about religion
and the philosophy of religion,
are always in trouble about how to define religion.
They can define Hinduism, Mohammedanism, Christianity, easily,
but Buddhism creates trouble.
They can define God as being the centre of all religion,
but then Buddhism becomes a problem.
They can define prayer as the essence of religion,
but again Buddhism creates trouble,
because there is no God and no prayer, no mantra, nothing.
You have only to be empty.
The concept of God will not allow you to be empty;
prayer will be a disturbance;
chanting will not allow you to be empty.
Simply being empty, everything happens.
Emptiness is the secret key of Buddhism.
You be in such a way that you are not.

Let me explain a little more about emptiness to you,
then it will be possible to go into this Zen anecdote.

Physicists have been working for three hundred years
to find the base, the substance of matter,
and the deeper they reached, the more they were puzzled.
Because the deeper they groped,
the less and less substantial matter was;
the less and less material matter was.
And when they really stumbled upon the source of matter,
they simply couldn't believe it,
because it was against all their conceptions.
It was not matter at all: it was simply energy.
Energy is non-substantial. It has no weight.
You cannot see it. You can only see the effects of it,
you can never see it directly.

Eddington, in 1930, said that we were in search of matter,

but now all new insight into matter
shows that there is no matter;
it looks more and more like a thought
and less and less like a thing.
Suddenly the insight of Buddha
became very, very significant again,
because Buddha did the same with human matter, the human stuff.
Physicists were trying to penetrate matter in an objective way
to find out what was there inside it,
and they found nothing. Total emptiness.
And the same was discovered by Buddha in his inner journey.
He was trying to find out who was there inside
—the substance of human consciousness—
but the more he penetrated, the more he became aware
that it becomes more and more empty.
And when he suddenly reached to the very core,
there was nothing.
All had disappeared. The house was empty.
And around this emptiness everything exists.
Emptiness is your soul,
so Buddha had to coin a new word which had never existed before.
With a new discovery you have to change your language.
New words have to be coined,
because you have revealed new truths
and old words cannot contain them.
Buddha had to create a new word.
In India people had always believed in the reality
of the soul, *atma,* but Buddha discovered
that there was no soul, no *atma.*
He had to coin a new word—*anatta. Anatta* means no-self.
The deepest hidden in you is emptiness—a state of no-self.
You are not; you only appear to be.

Let me explain to you in a different way
because it is one of the most difficult things to understand.
Even if you understand intellectually,
it is almost impossible to trust it.
You are not? Your being seems so taken for granted.
And you can always ask foolish questions.
Buddha was asked again and again:
If you are not, then who is speaking?
If you are not, then who becomes hungry?

Emptiness and the Monk's Nose 75

And who goes begging in the town?
If you are not, then who is standing before me?

The emperor Wu, in China, asked Bodhidharma immediately:
If you say that you are not and nothing is,
and emptiness is the very substance of your inner being,
then who is this fellow talking to me, standing before me?
Bodhidharma shrugged his shoulders and said: I don't know.

Nobody knows, and Buddha says that nobody can know,
because it is not a substance that you can encounter
as an object; it is no-substance, you cannot encounter it.
This Buddha calls realisation:
when you come to understand that the innermost emptiness
cannot be known, it is unknowable,
then you have become a realised man.

It is difficult, so let me again explain it to you.
You go to a movie. Something beautiful is happening there.
The screen is empty. Then the projector starts working.
The screen disappears
because the projected pictures hide it completely.
And what are these projected pictures?
Nothing but a play of light and shade.
You see somebody throwing a spear on the screen,
the spear moves fast. But what is happening exactly?
The movement is only an appearance, it is not happening.
It cannot happen. In fact a movie is not a movie at all,
because it has no movement; all the pictures are still.
But an appearance is created through a trick.
The trick is that many still pictures of the spear
in different positions are flashed on the screen
so fast that you cannot see the gap between two pictures—
and you have the feeling that the spear is moving.
I raise my hand. You take a hundred pictures of my hand
in different positions and then flash them so fast
that the eyes cannot catch the gap between two pictures.
Then you will see the hand being raised.
A hundred still pictures, or a million still pictures,
are projected and the movement is created.
And if the film is a three dimensional film
and somebody is throwing a spear,

you may be so much taken in by it, that you may lean
to the right or to the left to avoid the spear.
When three dimensional pictures
came into existence for the first time, they scared people.
With a horse running at you, you become afraid
because the horse is soon going to enter the hall;
and you may even lean to the right or left,
as the case may be, to avoid the clash.
The movement is false, it is not happening there,
it is just fast-moving still pictures.
And the falseness is not apparent unless you see the film
moving very slowly, being projected very slowly.

The same, in a different sense, is happening in life.
Thoughts are projected by your mind so fast
that you cannot see the gap between two thoughts.
The screen is completely covered by the thoughts
and they move so fast
that you cannot see that each thought is separate.
That's what Tilopa says:
Thoughts are like clouds,
without any roots, with no home.
And a thought is not related to another thought;
a thought is an individual unit,
just like dust particles, separate.
But they move so fast you cannot see the gap between.
You feel they have a unity, a certain association.

That association is a false notion,
but because of that association, ego is created.

Buddha says:
Fast-moving thoughts create an illusion,
as if there is some centre to them,
as if they are related to one thing.
They are not related, they are without roots—like clouds.
When you meditate you will understand that each single thought
is an individual thought, not related to another.
Between the two is the emptiness of your being.
They come and go, but they come and go so fast
that you cannot see the intervals. Ego is created.

And then you start feeling
that there is somebody as a centre in you

Emptiness and the Monk's Nose

to which everything belongs—thoughts, actions.
But Buddha says that there is nobody inside you.
When you go deeper you will understand the truth of it:
it is not a philosophical doctrine.

Buddha can be defeated very easily by argument;
he was thrown out of this country
because Indians are great arguers.
They have done nothing else for five thousand years
but argue, and through argument Buddha can be defeated
because the whole thing seems to be absurd.
Buddha is saying that there are actions, there is no actor;
there are thoughts, there is no thinker;
there is hunger, there is satiety;
there is illness, there is health;
but there is no centre to which they all belong.
They are just like clouds moving in an empty sky,
not related to each other at all.
Through experience nobody can defeat Buddha,
but through logic it is very simple.

Soon Buddha became aware that through logic
he could be defeated very easily. So what to do?
India had great scholars in those days,
great pundits, great logicians, hair-splitters.
So Buddha simply declared: I am not a metaphysician,
I am not a philosopher, and I have no doctrine to offer.
These are not conclusions of my intellect.
If somebody wants to understand them,
he will have to come and live with me,
and do whatsoever I say.
And after a year, if he lives with me silently in meditation,
then I am ready to argue with him, never before.

And it happened that although many great scholars came to him,
this was his condition.
Sariputta came. He was a very famous scholar,
and he had five hundred of his own disciples.
They were great scholars in their own right:
they knew all the Vedas, they knew all the Upanishads,
they knew all the wisdom of the centuries,
and they had very, very keen intellects.
Sariputta came and Buddha said:

You have come, that's good.
But for one year you have to remain silent,
because I have no doctrine to propose,
so there is no possibility of any argument.
I have something in my being to share,
but no doctrine to propose.
So, if you like, you can be here.

Then came Moulunkaputta, another great scholar,
and Buddha said the same to him:
For one year you sit silently by my side,
not raising a single question.
For one year you have to let your mind subside
and penetrate into the intervals.
After one year, exactly one year,
if you have some questions, I will answer.

Sariputta was also sitting there. He started laughing.
Moulunkaputta asked: What is the matter?
Why are you laughing?
Sariputta said: Don't be befooled by this man.
If you have to ask anything, ask immediately,
because after one year you will not be able to ask anything.
This has happened to me.
One year, meditating silently, questions disappeared.
One year, meditating silently,
the argumentative mind disappeared,
and the arguer disappeared.
One year, sitting by the side of this man, one becomes empty;
and then he laughs, and then he plays tricks,
and then then he says: Now you ask.
Where are your doctrines and principles and arguments?
And nothing arises inside.
So, Moulunkaputta, if you have to ask, right now is the moment—
otherwise, never.

Buddha said: I will fulfill my promise.
If you remain one year and if you have any questions,
I will answer, whatsoever the questions.
Moulunkaputta remained. One year passed.
He forgot completely about the year passing
and that the day had come back; but Buddha remembered.
After one year, on exactly the day, he said to Moulunkaputta:
Now you stand, Moulunkaputta, and you can ask.

Emptiness and the Monk's Nose

Moulunkaputta stood there silent, with closed eyes,
and then he said:
There is nothing to ask, and there is nobody to ask.
I have completely disappeared.

Buddhism is an experience
and Zen is the purest of all Buddha's teachings—
the very essence.
And the centre around which the whole experience moves
is emptiness.
How to become empty?
That is what meditation is all about:
how to become so silent, that you cannot even see yourself—
because that too is a disturbance.
Feeling that 'I am', is also a disturbance—even that goes.
One is completely effaced, utterly effaced.
The sheet is clean, it becomes like a summer sky—
clouds are no longer there, just the depth,
the infinite blueness, ending nowhere, beginning nowhere.
This is what Buddha calls the *anatta,*
the innermost centre of non-being, of no-self.
Buddha says: You walk, but there is no walker;
you eat, but there is no eater;
you are born, but there is nobody who is born.
You will be ill, and you will become old,
but there is nobody who becomes ill and becomes old.
And you will die, but there is nobody who dies.
And this is what eternal life is...
not being born, how can you die?
Not being there, how can you be ill or healthy?

These things happen, and if you become a deep witness to them,
by and by you will know that they happen on their own accord.
They are not concerned with you.
They are not in any way happening in relation to you.
Unrelated, homeless, rootless—
this is the utter enlightenment.

Knowing this, that things happen, like dreams,
one is not bothered this way or that,
one is neither happy nor unhappy. One simply is not.
Buddha says: You can never be happy, because,

in the very insistence that you are, unhappiness hides.
You can never be liberated, because you are the bondage.
Liberation is not of you, liberation is from you.

This is the deepest core ever touched, the deepest core.
Mahavir says: You will be enlightened.
Buddha says: You are the hindrance.
Mahavir says: You will live in *moksha,*
in the ultimate state of consciousness—
blissful, eternally blissful.
Buddha says: Unless you die,
you will never attain to that state.

You are the only barrier,
the only hindrance, the only obstacle.
When you are not, that state is.
That state is not yours,
you cannot claim it; in fact, because you are,
you don't allow that state to be.
It is already here within you, this very moment,
but you don't allow it to function.
You try to control it, manipulate it.
The ego is the great manipulator, the controller,
and the whole effort of all the Buddhas
is how to drop the control.
Once the control is dropped, the controller disappears.
That is what I am trying to do with you
with these many meditations.
The effort is how to drop the control,
how to drop the great manipulator.

You whirl in a Dervish dance.
In the beginning you are there.
Soon you feel nausea,
but that nausea is not only physical,
it is deeply spiritual.
You start feeling nausea when the moment comes
for control to be dropped.
When that moment nears, you start feeling nausea.
The nausea is that the control is being lost.
You feel dizzy; you feel that you may fall down.
These are not just physical things—
deep inside the ego is feeling as if it is being thrown

Emptiness and the Monk's Nose

off the track. The ego is feeling dizzy.
It is feeling that if this whirling continues
for even a little longer, I will not be able to be there.
You start to feel like vomiting.
In fact, that vomit is not only physical,
just one part is physical,
a deeper part is the vomit of the ego.
If you continue to feel disturbed,
there will be a physical vomiting,
but if you don't bother about it,
soon physical vomiting will disappear.
And then the real vomit will happen:
one day, suddenly, the ego is vomited.
Suddenly an ugly phenomenon within you escapes;
suddenly the disease from you is thrown out;
suddenly you are ego-free.
It happens unexpectedly.
When it happens for the first time, you cannot even believe it;
you cannot believe that, without the ego, you are.
There is nobody inside, and you are;
and you are so perfect and so beautiful and so blissful—
without anybody being there!

The ego has to be thrown off-centre,
because it has become so deeply rooted in your mind,
through many lives.
It has usurped the whole being;
emptiness has been thrown into the background,
into the unconscious, and the ego has usurped the throne.
Now the ego has become the king,
and it goes on manipulating everything.

This parable, this small anecdote, will tell you many things
about how the ego can be thrown off-centre.

Sekkyo said to one of his monks:
Can you grab hold of emptiness?
I'll try, said the monk,
and he cupped his hands in the air.

The master is playing a trick.
The master asked: Can you get hold of emptiness?

The question is tricky,
and if the disciple was of any understanding,
he would not have tried.
The very effort to catch hold of emptiness is stupid.
You can catch hold of something,
you cannot catch hold of nothing.
How can you catch hold of nothing?
The disciple still feels that emptiness is something;
he still feels that emptiness is not empty—
it is a name, a label of something which can be caught hold of.
If he had a little understanding, even a little understanding,
he would have done something else than catch hold of emptiness.
That was the test.

There are stories where a master asks a disciple:
Can you get hold of emptiness?
and the disciple seizes the master's nose
and gives it a great yank—
that would have been absolutely right.
Because the question is absurd.
Whatsoever you try
it is going to fail from the very beginning.
Nothing will help.

These are the Zen koans.
A Zen master gives you an absurd problem,
which cannot be solved.
There is no answer to it.

I have heard about a toy-shop somewhere in America.
A father was purchasing a toy puzzle for his child.
He tried to fix it, and he tried and tried in many ways,
but something was always wrong,
it wouldn't work.
So he asked the manager of the shop:
If even I cannot make head or tail out of this,
how do you suppose that a small child will be able to?
The manager said: Nobody can do it.
This is just to give the child a taste of modern life.
It is not meant to be, nobody can do it, it cannot be fixed.
The part, the different parts, are not made to fix.

This was just to give a taste of modern life:

Emptiness and the Monk's Nose

whatsoever you do, nothing is of any avail,
in the end you will feel frustrated.
Do this or that, there are millions of alternatives,
but all are false, because they fail from the very beginning.
The puzzle was not a puzzle, but an absurdity.
A puzzle is that which can be solved by some intelligence.
An absurdity is that which by its very nature is not solvable,
cannot be solved. A koan is an absurd puzzle.

The master says: Can you get hold of emptiness?
Now, from the very beginning, any solution is debarred.
In the very wording of the question
he has created an absurdity.
How can you catch hold of nothing?
You can of course, catch hold of something.
But nothing? Emptiness?
All your efforts are doomed from the very beginning.
And this is the whole thing:
the master is trying to help the disciple to become aware,
but the ego takes the problem immediately
and starts trying to solve it. It becomes a challenge.

That's why so many people try a crossword puzzle,
this and that.
Just looking at the newspaper their ego is challenged;
they have to solve it, otherwise it will haunt them.
They are so intelligent, how can this puzzle exist?
They will have to solve it, it becomes an obsession.
Millions of people waste millions of hours
solving foolish things.
The ego takes up the challenge.

When the master said: Can you get hold of emptiness?
he was exciting the ego,
and ego is the most stupid thing in human life.
You can excite it by anything—by anything.

At an advertisement in the newspaper:
Do you have a two-car garage, or only a one-car garage?—
immediately the ego feels disturbed
because other people have a two-car garage,
and you have only one. Your life is wasted.
You existed for nothing. Move fast, borrow money.
Do something! Even if you get ulcers on the way, it is okay.

Cancer one can tolerate,
but one cannot tolerate a one-car garage.
Commit suicide, but you have to have a two-car garage.
Ego is the most stupid thing,
and the whole market of salesmen and advertisers
depends on your ego.
They excite the ego: they exploit you.
And it is difficult to prevent them unless you drop the ego.
They will go on and on. A big car becomes an ego symbol.

I have heard that Mulla Nasrudin went to America.
In his town he had never seen a bigger car than a Fiat.
When he saw such big cars he was simply puzzled:
What to call them? Because they are not cars,
and they are not buses; and in such a big car
only one person sits or a dog. What is the matter?
He saw such big houses—what to call them?
In his town a two-storey house is called an *atari*, a palace.
Then he saw a hundred-storied house. His mind boggled.
You cannot call it a house, you cannot call it a palace—
there simply exists no word for it.

And then he saw Niagara.
He closed his eyes and he said:
It seems I am seeing a dream.
He had seen small waterfalls, his town had a waterfall,
but it ran only in the rainy season. What is this?
And he became so puzzled that it was even impossible
to appreciate such big, tremendous things;
and he was not able to say anything to the guide.
So then he started feeling guilty—he should say something.

Then they came across a small river.
So Mulla Nasrudin thought: This is the opportunity.
And he said: It seems somebody's car radiator is leaking.

Things go on becoming bigger and bigger and bigger
just because of the ego. They are not needed.
There exists no necessity for them.
Life becomes more and more complex because of the stupid ego.
And once it takes the challenge,
it is always ready to take it,
without even asking if this is possible, impossible,

rational, irrational.

The master Sekkyo said:
Can you grab hold of emptiness?
I'll try, said the monk.

This is the answer of the ego: I will try.
It takes all sorts of challenges
and a koan is a great challenge.
It is made in such a way that you cannot solve it.
And trying to solve it, you will become aware
that your very effort to solve it is idiotic.
In trying to solve it, you will become aware
that you have taken the challenge. That was wrong.
The one who says within you: I will try and I will do,
is impotent.

A koan is given to a disciple to feel the impotency
—that you cannot do—
to feel the helplessness,
because the ego can disappear only in a helpless state,
otherwise not.
The ego can disappear only when it is a total failure;
when not even a slight possibility of its success exists.
Only then, otherwise it can go on hoping
that it will do something else, or something else,
and it will try this alternative and that.
There must exist a possibility for the emptiness to be caught,
for you to catch hold of it:
I will try.
Remember always to watch before you say: I will try.
Don't allow the ego to come in.
Just watch. Be intelligent, don't be egoistic.
Intelligence is good. Being egoistic
in fact hinders the functioning of your intelligence.
Such a simple thing.
The disciple should have hit the master, right then and there:
What type of nonsense are you telling me?

But people have tried to solve all sorts of nonsense,
because the ego says: There must be some way.
The ego says: If the problem exists, the solution must exist.
What is the necessity? You can create a problem,
but there is no necessity in nature for the solution to exist.

And, as I have observed, ninety-nine per cent
of the problems of philosophy are foolish.
They cannot be solved,
but great minds are involved in solving them.
For example, simple problems like: Who created the world?
are foolish, but great theologians,
religious people, scholars, waste their whole life on them.
For thousands of years many have been worried
about who created the world.
And it cannot be solved; it is a koan.
It is absurd, because the very question is such,
the nature of it is such, that whatsoever you do,
it will again jump up and stand on its feet,
it will not be killed.

For example, if you say:
A created the world,
immediately the question is there:
Who created A? B created A.
Then the question is there:
Who created B? You go on, and on, and finally,
just fed up with the whole thing, you will have to say:
This Z, nobody created this Z.
But why get to Z? Why not say in the first place
that nobody created this world? Why go from A to Z?
When you have to concede that nobody created God,
then why say that God created the world?
If God can exist without being created,
then why not this existence?
There seems to be no reason.
But people go on, and they think
that they are doing very serious religious thinking.
This is not religious thinking at all;
in fact, no thinking is religious.
Non-thinking is religious.

Can you get hold of emptiness? What nonsense!
Emptiness is nothing, how can you get hold of it?
It has no boundaries, no limitations to it,
it is not possible, but the ego says: I will try.
I'll try, said the monk,
and he cupped his hands in the air.
Not only did he say it, he tried—

Emptiness and the Monk's Nose

he cupped his hands in the air.
You may think that you would have done better.
What would you do? Whatsoever you do will be the same.
Without knowing what you would do, I say it will be the same.
You jump this way and that, and try to catch hold—
you will simply look foolish.

...and he cupped his hands in the air.

That's not very good, said Sekkyo,
You haven't got anything there.

There is something to be understood here—
if your hands are open, emptiness is there;
if your hands are not open, and you have made a fist,
emptiness has disappeared.
In a fist there is no space;
in an open hand the whole sky is there,
but it is in an open hand.
The meaning is very subtle, but very beautiful—
if you try to catch hold of it you will miss,
if you don't try it is already there.
If you don't try, in your open hand the whole sky exists;
nothing less than that.
If you try to catch hold of the sky,
and you make a fist out of your hand,
everything has disappeared.

What is there in your fist?
Maybe a little stale air—
and that too shows that the fist is not exactly complete.
That's why. If the fist is exactly complete,
the whole sky has disappeared from it.

The ultimate is already there;
no effort is needed to get it.
In the very effort you miss and lose and go astray.

One man came to Lin Chi, a great Zen master,
and said: I am very troubled.
I would like to become a Buddha myself. What to do?
Lin Chi chased him out with his staff, out of the temple.
He hit him hard, the man started running,
and he chased him out of the temple.

Somebody who was standing by said:
This is too hard. The poor man has not asked anything wrong.
He was simply asking a very religious question,
and he looked very sincere—
you should have looked at his eyes, his face.
He had really travelled a long way to come to you,
and he was asking a simple, sincere, religious question:
how to become a Buddha. And what you did
seems to be too hard on the poor man, and unjustified.
Lin Chi said: I chased him out
because he was asking an absurd thing.
He is already a Buddha. If he tries, he will miss.
And if he can understand why I hit him and chased him out,
then he should leave all effort—
there is nothing to be achieved, he has just to be himself.
He has to be just whatsoever he is.

Be loose and natural, what Tilopa says,
and then Buddha is already there in the inner shrine.
One has not to become a Buddha, one is always born a Buddha.
Buddhahood is your innermost essential nature.
You need not enquire about it: you need not try for it.

The poor seeker went to another master,
thinking that this Lin Chi was mad:
I ask a simple question and he hits me hard,
and then chases me out of the temple.
He is completely insane.
He went to another master, a master who was opposed to Lin Chi.
They had their monasteries nearby in the same hills.
He went there. He felt:
This man will be right, because he is opposed to Lin Chi.
And now I know why he is opposed.

He went to the master, the other master
and asked the same question. The master said:
Have you ever been before to any other master?
He said: Yes. But it was wrong of me to go there.
I went to see Lin Chi. He hit me hard,
and chased me out of the temple.
Suddenly, the master became very ferocious,
as if he would kill him.
He pulled his sword out of his sheath, and the man ran away.
The master said: What do you think?

Do you think I am an ignorant man?
If Lin Chi can do that, I will kill you completely.

He asked somebody on the way what to do. The man said:
You go back to Lin Chi, he is more compassionate.
And he did.
When he went back Lin Chi asked: Why have you come back?
He said: The other man is dangerous, more dangerous than you.
He would have completely killed me.
He seems to be a maniac, ferocious.
Lin Chi said: We help each other. It is a conspiracy.
Now you be here and never again ask how to be a Buddha,
because you are already.
One has just to live. You live like a Buddha.
You don't bother, don't try to become one.
And he became enlightened.

This is the greatest teaching possible: you live it out.
And this is what I would like you to do also.
You live it out—
you need not bother to become, you are already.
And Buddhahood is a being, it is never a becoming.
You can never become. How can you become a Buddha?
Either you are, or you are not.
How can you become?
How can an ordinary stone become a diamond?
Either it is or it is not; becoming is not possible.
So you decide: either you are, or you are not.
If you are not, forget everything about it.
If you are, there is no need to think about it.
In either way you simply be whatsoever you are,
and in that very being everything is caught hold of—
you can catch hold of emptiness without any effort.

That's not very good, said Sekkyo,
You haven't got anything there.

Well, master, said the monk,
please show me a better way.

There are no ways better or worse.
The way doesn't exist,

because the way means that something has to become.
The way means that some distance has to be travelled.
The way means that you and the goal are separate.
The way is possible if I am travelling to come to you,
the way is possible if you are travelling to come to me,
but how is the way possible if I am trying to be myself?
There is no distance.

If you are trying to reach yourself, the way is not possible.
There is no space, no distance.
You are already yourself, the way doesn't exist.
That is why Zen is called the pathless path, the gateless gate.
The gate is not there, and this is the gate.
The pathless path—the path doesn't exist,
and to understand this, is the path.
The Zen effort is to throw you onto your reality immediately.
There is no need to postpone.

Well, master, said the monk,
please show me a better way.
He is still in the same trap. The ego is asking:
Then something else may be possible;
maybe something else can be done
and you can catch hold of emptiness.
Thereupon, Sekkyo seized the monk's nose
and gave it a great yank.

Why are Zen masters so rude?
And only Zen masters are so rude.
They have a real compassion,
and you can be thrown to yourself only in such a way,
there is no other way. You need an electric shock.
You need shock treatment. Why shock treatment?
Because only in a shock, for a small portion of time,
does your thinking stop, otherwise not.
Only in a shock can you become aware, alert, your sleep drops.
Otherwise you are a sleepwalker.
Unless somebody hits you hard, your sleep cannot be broken.

Thereupon, Sekkyo seized the monk's nose
and gave it a great yank.

Ouch! yelled the monk, you hurt me!

Emptiness and the Monk's Nose

In this 'Ouch!' is the whole mystery.
Somebody yanks on your nose—what happens inside?
The first thing is that it was never expected.
The monk was expecting some intellectual answer.
This is rather total.
He was asking for some theory,
some doctrine, some method, technique:
he wanted a head-to-head communication.
This is rather total. The total master jumps on him,
just like a cat jumps on a mouse. A total thing.
The whole cat jumps, not the head;
and the whole mouse is caught, not the head.
This is a total thing, unexpected.
And unexpectedness is the key,
because if the mind can expect, there will be no shock.
If the mind can expect, then the mind is already dead.
So if you go to Sekkyo, remember well—
he will not do the same to you again,
because you can expect it now.
He will do something absolutely unexpected.

Because Zen masters hit, throw people out of the window,
jump on them, do anything,
it has sometimes happened in the history of Zen
that people will come completely ready.
Dimensions are limited.
What can you do? You can hit, you can throw,
you can jump on the man. Just a few alternatives are there.
So people will come completely ready.
But you cannot deceive a master—he will not do anything;
he will simply sit silently—and that will be unexpected.

Unexpectedness is the key, because in an unexpected moment
the mind cannot function. That's what 'Ouch!' means.
The mind has simply stopped.
This voice doesn't come from the mind,
it comes from your totality.
It is not manipulated by the ego,
because there is no time for the ego to manipulate.
It has happened so suddenly,
the master has jumped upon you so suddenly,
there was no time to prepare, to get ready, to do something.
This 'Ouch!' comes from your whole body, mind, soul;

from your very depth of emptiness it comes,
it has a flavour of the total.

And there is no manipulator,
nobody has done it—it has happened.
And when something happens and the doer is not,
that is how emptiness is caught,
that is how you catch hold of emptiness.
This is emptiness. This 'Ouch!' comes from the inner emptiness.
Nobody is a doer of it.
The disciple has not done it: it has simply happened.
And in that happening, in that 'Ouch!' mind is not functioning.
It has passed through the mind,
but it has not come from the mind.
And it has passed through the mind at such a fast speed...
in fact, if you are really hurt on the nose, yanked,
the 'Ouch!' that happens breaks the sound-barrier.
You go and ask the physiologists: it moves faster than sound.
It has a total energy in it and it is beautiful,
because this man may have completely forgotten
the spontaneousness of being.
He is thrown back to his spontaneousness.
He is thrown from the mind
deeper into his own innermost shrine:
from there comes this 'Ouch!'
Unexpected, not doing it, it happens.
It happens out of emptiness, you have caught hold.

Ouch! yelled the monk, You hurt me!
And immediately comes back the echo: You hurt me.
It lasts only for a single moment, not even a single moment,
a minute part of it, a glimpse, a lightning,
and immediately the mind takes control again: You hurt me.

Look at these three words—you, hurt, me.
This is the whole of life: you and me and the hurt.
Immediately the whole mind is back,
with all the basic elements: you, me and the hurt.

That's the way to get hold of emptiness,
said Sekkyo.

He has revealed it.
He has not explained, he has already given it.

Emptiness and the Monk's Nose

He has not only indicated,
he has created a situation in which it happened.
That's what a master is for:
to create a situation in which things happen to you,
to create a situation in which you can become aware
of the mechanicalness of the mind,
and of the spontaneousness of your inner no-self.
And then you can move, by and by, from the mind
to the inner spontaneousness.
You can become loose and natural.
You have to understand that everything can go on
without your mind trying to manipulate—
everything in fact goes on very beautifully.
The trouble starts when you take hold,
when you try to manipulate,
when you want the mind to be in the saddle—
then the trouble starts.
Otherwise everything goes on, and goes on so beautifully.
There is no need to improve it, and you cannot improve it.

The master gave him a glimpse of his inner being,
because the 'Ouch!' came from the very centre.
It was not of the body, not of the mind.
It was of the total, and in that moment
he functioned as a spontaneous being, not as a doer.

This functioning can become your whole life—
that's what religion should be.
A religious life is a functioning of the spontaneous being.
There are situations every moment.
You act, but not as a doer, you act spontaneously.
Somebody smiles, what do you do?
You can smile as a doer, you can manipulate;
you can smile because it will be impolite if you don't smile;
you can smile, because in a society you have to exist
and this man is very important. In fact,
it is greatly flattering that he smiled at you, so you have to.
It may be a bargain, a business, a trade, a social mannerism,
or it may be simply an unconscious habit.
Somebody smiles—you react, you smile.
A push-button smile, your being is absolutely unaffected.
In fact, you are not in your smile at all.
It is just on the lips, a painted thing:

just an exercise of the lips, nothing in it, absolutely empty.
You manipulate.

It happened that once I stayed in a house
and the man of the house died.
He had no wife, so his sister came to help arrange things.
And I was staying there and was simply watching
what was happening. Whenever somebody came
the sister would look out of the door
and immediately she would start crying and weeping
and saying things about the dead man:
that he was so beautiful
and he is gone and her whole life will be now sad,
a light has disappeared—and everything!
And she would do it so mechanically;
immediately saying something if somebody was coming.
She in fact told me: You sit more outside in the garden.
If somebody comes simply give me a knock.

And when the person had gone, she was perfectly okay.
Tears were flowing down her cheeks
when she was crying and weeping,
but as soon as the man was out of the house,
his back towards the house,
the tears would disappear and she was perfectly okay,
talking and chatting and doing things.
I was simply surprised. I asked: How do you do it?
You could have been a perfect actress.
You simply do it so perfectly that even the tears come down!

Manipulation. You are not only manipulating another's body,
you are manipulating your own body—
and this goes on and on continuously.
All spontaneity is lost; you become a robot.
This is how life becomes ugly, crippled;
this is how a hell is created.
Then your love is false, your hate is false,
your smile is false, your tears are false.
And how do you suppose
to live in such falsity and think of bliss;
to live in such falsity and think of truth;
to live in such falsity and think of liberation, *moksha*?
There is no *moksha* for a false being. Falsity should drop.

Emptiness and the Monk's Nose

Be spontaneous, there is nothing to lose
and everything to be gained.

In the beginning you may sometimes feel a little awkward
because you wanted to smile,
it was needed as a social mannerism
but a spontaneous smile was not there.
But only in the beginning.
Soon your authenticity will be felt by others also,
and soon your authenticity will start paying you.
It pays so tremendously, that when a real smile
comes to your lips, it will be as total as the 'Ouch!'—
the whole being smiles, the whole being becomes a smile.
All around you your smile spreads like ripples in consciousness.
Everybody who is near you will feel a purity,
a bath-like purity,
and you will feel a tremendous bliss happening to you.

A simple act of authentic spontaneity,
and immediately you are transported
from this world to another world.

Love—or even anger...
I tell you that even positive emotions, false, are ugly;
and even negative emotions, authentic, are beautiful.
Even anger is beautiful when your whole being feels it,
when every fibre of your being is vibrant with it.
Look at a small child angry—
and then you will feel the beauty of it.
His whole being is in it.
Radiant. His face red. Such a small child looks so powerful
that it seems he could destroy the whole world!
And what happens to a child once he is angry?
After a few minutes, a few seconds, everything is changed
and he is happy and dancing and running around the house again.
Why doesn't this happen to you?
You move from one falsity to another.
Really, anger is not a lasting phenomenon,
by its very nature it is a momentary thing.
If the anger is real, it lasts for a few moments;
and while it lasts, authentic, it is beautiful.
It harms nobody. A real, spontaneous thing
cannot harm anybody. Only falsity harms.
In a man who can be angry spontaneously,

the tide goes after a few seconds
and he relaxes perfectly to the very other extreme.
He becomes infinitely loving.
This anger has not destroyed love.
No authentic anger ever destroys love.
On the contrary, it creates it again and again, renews it.

If a wife and husband never get angry,
you can be certain there exists no love between them.
That's absolutely certain.
But if sometimes they get angry, really angry,
that anger refreshes everything.
In fact, after the anger is gone
they will again have a new honeymoon.
Now everything is fresh, the storm has passed,
it has cleaned everything. Again they are new.
They moved away, now they fall in love again.
To fall in love again and again and again is the eternity of love.
If there is no anger, real anger,
if you are boiling within and just go on with a smile
on the face because you are a husband and she is a wife
and anger will create trouble—
if now you smile, that smile is false.
And the wife knows that your smile is false;
and you also know that her smile is false.
In the house you live a false life.
And this falsity becomes so ingrained
that you have completely lost track of what a real smile is,
of what a real kiss is, of what a real embrace is,
you have completely lost track.
Then you go through the motions—you embrace your wife,
you kiss her, and you think of other things.
You move through the motions
but they are gestures, impotent, dead.
How can your life be a fulfillment?

And I tell you that even negative emotions are good, if real;
and if they are real, by and by, their very reality
transforms them. They become more and more positive
and a moment comes when all positivity and negativity disappears.
You simply remain authentic:
you don't know what is good and what is bad,
you don't know what is positive and what is negative.

Emptiness and the Monk's Nose

You are simply authentic.

This authenticity will allow you to have a glimpse of the real.
Only the real can know the real,
the true can know the truth,
the authentic can know the authentic that surrounds you.

That's the way to get hold of emptiness.

The master created a situation, allowed the disciple
to move in a spontaneous act, howsoever small—
just 'Ouch!' and lightning happens.
This can become a satori, the first enlightenment.

So remember a few things:
you have to move from the mechanical to the spontaneous;
from the mental, the verbal, to the non-mental, the non-verbal;
from the part to the total;
from the false to the real;
and from the ego to the non-ego—from the self to the no-self.
Already the no-self exists by the side of yourself.
Just a change of attention, a change of gear is needed.
The non-mechanical exists by the side of the mechanical,
the real is always waiting by the side of the false—
just a change of gestalt,
just a look towards the spontaneous is needed.
Try it for twenty-four hours.
Whenever you have an opportunity to move
from the false to the real,
from the mechanical to the authentic,
immediately change the gear.
And remain floating as if you are an emptiness,
don't try to control yourself too much.
Remain loose and natural.

The Cataract at Luliang
24th February 1975

Confucius was looking at the cataract at Luliang.
It falls from a height of two hundred feet,
and its foam reaches fifteen miles away.
No scaly finny creature could survive therein.

Yet Confucius saw an old man go in.
Thinking the old man was suffering from some trouble
and was therefore desirous of ending his life,
Confucius bade a disciple run along the bank
to try to save him.

The old man emerged about a hundred paces off,
and with flowing hair, he went caroling along the bank.

Confucius followed him, and when he caught up with him he said:
I had thought, sir, you were a spirit,
but now I see you are a man. Kindly tell me,
is there any way to deal thus with the water?

No, replied the man, I have no way;
plunging in with the whirl, I come out with the swirl.
I accommodate myself to the water, not the water to me.
And so I am able to deal with it after this fashion.

You have a thousand and one problems,
and you try to solve them.
But not even a single problem is solved.
It cannot be solved, because in the first place
there are not a thousand and one problems, there is only one;
and if you see a thousand and one problems,
you will not be able to see the one that really is.
You go on seeing things which are not, and, because of that,
you miss seeing that which is.

So the first thing to be understood
is the basic, the only problem. It is perennial,
it doesn't belong in particular to you, or to me,

or to somebody else. It belongs to man as such.
It is born with you and, unfortunately, as is the situation
with millions of people, the problem will die with you.
If the problem can die before you die
you have become enlightened.
And the whole effort of religion
is to help you to dissolve the problem
before it has killed you completely.

There is a possibility of a man without any problems,
and that is the religious man. He has no problems,
because he has solved the basic problem. He has cut the root.

That's why Tilopa says: Cut the root of the mind.
Don't go on cutting the leaves and the branches.
There are millions, and, by cutting them,
you will not be able to cut the root,
and the tree will go on growing.
It will become even denser and thicker and bigger
if you go on pruning the leaves.
Simply forget about the leaves. They are not the problems.
The problem is somewhere in the root. Cut the root,
and the tree by and by disappears, withers away.

So where is the root problem of the mind?
It is neither yours, nor anybody else's;
it belongs to man as such.
It comes into existence the moment you are born,
but it can dissolve before you die.
A child is born...

Follow me step by step,
if you can understand the problem rightly,
it is solved immediately,
because the problem carries its own solution within it.
The problem is like a seed
and the solution is like a flower that is hidden in the seed.
If you can understand the seed correctly, totally,
the solution is already there. To solve a problem
is in fact not to solve it, but to understand it.
The solution is not external to it, it is intrinsic.
It is hidden in it. So don't look for solutions,
just look deeper into the problem. Find the root.
In fact, there is no need even to cut.

Once you have understood it,
the very understanding becomes the cutting of the root.
So, follow me step by step to see how the problem is born.
And don't be concerned with the solution—
that's how philosophy arises in the world.
There is a problem, the mind starts to find some solution.
Philosophy arises.
There is a problem, the mind tries to understand it,
religion is born.

...a child is born and the child is absolutely helpless,
particularly the human child.
He cannot survive without others' help.
So this is the first thing:
no problem exists for animals and trees and birds.
They live a non-problematic life. They simply live
without any problems, anxiety, ulcers, cancer:
they simply live and enjoy
and celebrate the moment while they are.
They have no problem in their life
and they have no problem in their death—
they live a non-problematic existence.
Only a human child is born helpless.
All other children, animals, trees, birds,
can survive without the parents,
can survive without society,
can survive without a family.
Even if sometimes help is needed, it is very little,
a few days, at the most a few months.
But a human child is so helpless; for years he has to depend,
and it is there that the root has to be sought.

Why does helplessness create the human problem?
The child is helpless, he depends on others;
but the ignorant mind of the child
interprets this dependence on others
as if he is the centre of the whole world.

The child thinks:
Whenever I cry, my mother runs immediately;
whenever I am hungry, just an indication,
and the breast is given.
Whenever I am wet, just a slight crying, weeping,

and somebody comes and changes my clothes.
The child lives like an emperor.
In fact he is absolutely helpless and dependent,
and the mother and the father and the family
are all helping him to survive.
They are not dependent on the child,
the child is dependent on them.
But the ignorant mind of the child interprets it
as if he is the centre of the whole world,
as if the whole world exists for him.
And the whole world
is, of course, very small in the beginning:
the mother, on the fringe the father—this is the whole world.
And they both love the child.

The child becomes more and more egoistic.
He feels himself to be the very centre of all existence.
The ego is created.
Through dependence, helplessness, the ego is created.

In fact the situation is just the contrary,
there is no reason to create the ego.
But the child is absolutely ignorant,
and he is not capable of understanding
the complexity of the thing: he cannot feel he is helpless.
He feels he is the dictator.
And then for his whole life he will try to remain the dictator.
He will become a Napoleon, an Alexander, an Adolf Hitler—
your presidents, prime ministers, dictators, are all childish.
They are trying for the same thing,
they want to be the centre of the whole existence:
with them the world should live,
with them the world should die;
the whole world is their periphery
and they are the meaning of it,
the very meaning of life is hidden in them.
The child, of course,
naturally finds this interpretation correct,
because when the mother looks at him,
in the eyes of the mother he sees
that he is the significance of her life.
And when the father comes home he feels
that he is the very meaning of the life of the father.

The Cataract at Luliang

This lasts for three or four years—
and the four years of the beginning of life
are the most important; never again will there be
such a potential time in life.
Psychologists say that after the first four years
the child is almost complete.
The whole pattern is fixed; throughout his whole life
he will repeat the same pattern in different situations.
But the pattern is there already, complete.
By the seventh year the child is perfect:
now nothing else is going to happen to him.
He has all his attitudes confirmed, his ego settled.
Now he moves into the world, and then everywhere
there will be problems, millions of problems.
And he carries the root within him.

Once out of the circle of the family, problems will arise.
Because nobody bothers as your mother bothered about you;
nobody is concerned as your father was concerned with you.
There is total indifference. And the ego is hurt.
But now the pattern is set.
Whether hurt or not the child cannot change the pattern,
it has become the very blueprint of his being.
He will play with other children and try to dominate.
He will go to school and try to dominate,
try to come first in class, to become the most important man.
And he believes he is the 'superior-most',
but other children believe also in the same way.
There is conflict, there are egos in fight, struggle.

Then this becomes the whole story of life:
there are millions of egos around you, just like yours,
and everybody is trying to control, manoeuvre, domineer—
through wealth, power, politics, knowledge, strength,
lies, pretensions, hypocrisies, even religion, morality.
And everybody is trying to dominate,
to show the whole world that 'I am the centre'.
And this is the root of all problems.

Because of this concept, you are always
in conflict and struggle, with somebody or other.
Not that others are enemies to you,
everybody is just like you, in the same boat;

the plight is the same for everybody else.
They have been brought up in the same way.

There exists a certain school of psycho-analysts in the West
who have proposed that,
unless children are brought up without their father and mother,
the world will never be at peace.
I don't support them—
because then they will never be brought up in any way.
They have something of a truth in their proposal,
but it is a very dangerous proposal.
Because if children are brought up in nurseries
without fathers and mothers, without any love,
with total indifference, they may not have the problem
of the ego, but they will have some other problems,
in the same way dangerous, even more so.

If a child is brought up in total indifference
he will have no centre in him.
He will be a hotch-potch being, clumsy,
not knowing who he is. He will not have any identity.
Afraid, scared, he will not be able to take
even a single step without fear, because nobody loved him.
Of course, the ego will not be there, but, without the ego,
he will have no centre. He will not become a Buddha;
he will be just a dull, inferior being,
stupid and always feeling afraid.
Love is needed to make you feel fearless,
that you are accepted, that somebody loves you,
that you are not useless,
that you cannot be discarded in the junkyard.
If children are brought up in such a situation,
where love is lacking, they will not have egos, that's right.
Their life will not have so much struggle and fight.
But they will not be able to fight at all,
and they will be always in flight, escaping;
escaping from everybody, hiding in caves in their own being.
They will not be Buddhas,
they will not be radiant with vitality,
they will not be centred, at ease, at home.
They will simply be eccentric, off-centre.
That will not be a good situation either.

So I don't support these psycho-analysts.
They will create robots, not human beings—
robots of course have no problems.
They may create human beings like animals;
there will be less anxiety, less ulcers, less cancer.
But that is not worth achieving.
Then you are not growing to a higher peak of consciousness,
you are falling downwards. It is regression.
Of course, if you become an animal, there will be less anguish,
because there will be less consciousness.
And, if you become a stone, a rock,
there will be no anxiety at all
because there is nobody inside to feel anxious,
to feel anguish. But this is not worth achieving.
One has to be god-like, not rock-like.

And the meaning of the word 'God' is this:
to have absolute consciousness
and still have no worries, no anxieties, no problems;
to enjoy life like birds,
and to have a consciousness that is absolutely perfect;
to celebrate life like birds, to sing like birds—
not by regression,
but by growing to the optimum of consciousness.

The child gathers ego—it is natural,
nothing can be done about it, I accept it.
Only later on there is no need to carry it.

That ego is needed in the beginning
for the child to feel that he is accepted, loved, welcomed;
that he is a guest, not uninvited, invited.
The father, the mother, the family, the warmth around,
help him to grow strong, rooted, grounded.
It is needed, the ego gives him a protection.
It is good. It is just like the shell of a seed.
But the shell should not become the ultimate thing,
otherwise the seed will die.
The protection can become too much,
then it becomes a prison.
The protection must remain a protection,
and when the moment comes for the shell, the hard shell

of the seed to die into the earth, it should die naturally
so that the seed can sprout and life can be born.

The ego is just a protective shell—
the child needs it because he is helpless;
the child needs it because he is weak;
the child needs it because he is vulnerable
and there are millions of forces all around.
He needs a protection, a home, a base.
The whole world may be indifferent,
but he can always look towards the home,
from there he can gather significance.

But with significance comes the ego. He becomes egoistic.
And with this ego arises all the problems,
the thousand and one problems.
This ego will not allow you to fall in love
and millions of problems will arise in your life.
This ego would like everybody to surrender to you;
this ego will not allow you to surrender to anybody—
and love happens only when you surrender.
When you force somebody to surrender,
it is hate, destruction, it is not love.

And if there is no love,
your life will be without warmth, without any poetry in it.
It may be a plain prose, mathematical, logical, rational.
But how can one live without poetry?
Prose is okay, it is utilitarian, needed,
but it can never be life
because it can never be a celebration, it can never be festive.
And when life is not festive, it is boredom.
Poetry is needed, but for poetry you need surrender.
You need to throw off this ego.
If you can do it, put it aside, even for moments,
your life will have glimpses of the beautiful, of the Divine.
Without poetry you cannot really live, you can only exist.
Love is poetry.

And if love is not possible, how can you pray?
Then prayer becomes almost impossible,
and, without prayer, you will remain just a body,
you will never become aware of the innermost soul.
Only in prayer do you reach to the peaks.

Prayer is the highest peak of experience,
but love opens the door.
Prayer allows you into the innermost mystery of life.
When you cannot pray, then millions of problems arise.

Carl Gustav Jung, after a whole life
of studying thousands of people,
thousands of cases of people ill,
psychologically defective, psychologically confused,
said in his last testament:
I have never come across a psychologically ill person
whose real problem after the fortieth year is not religion.
After the fortieth year...
it is just like after the fourteenth year every boy and girl
will have to tackle sex—and there will be problems.
And if you tackle them wrongly,
then those problems will continue, hovering around you.

Exactly as sex becomes mature at the age of fourteen,
so a new dimension opens at the age of forty-two.
Because every seven years there are biological,
psychological and spiritual changes in your being—
every seven years.
Childhood is finished by the seventh year,
by the fourteenth, adolescence is gone,
by the twenty-first there are changes—every seventh year.
There is a rhythm in life.
By the year forty-two a new dimension arises,
the dimension of prayer, the religious dimension.
And, if you cannot tackle it rightly,
if you don't know what to do, you will be ill,
you will lose all rest, you will become restless.

If you cannot love at the age of fourteen,
you will not be able to pray at the age of forty-two.

You have been missing,
and the whole growth is a continuity.
If you miss one step, it becomes discontinuous.
The child gathers ego—he cannot love,
and he cannot be at ease with anybody.
The ego is constantly in fight.
You may be sitting silently,

but the ego is constantly in fight, just looking,
watching how to dominate, how to become dictatorial,
how to become the most supreme-most person in the world.

This creates problems everywhere.
In friendship, sex, prayer, love, society,
everywhere you are in conflict.
Even with the parents who have given this ego to you
there is conflict.
It is rarely that a son forgives his father,
rarely that a woman forgives her mother. Rarely.

Gurdjieff had a sentence written in his room
where he used to see the people.
It is simply unbelievable that a man like Gurdjieff
should write such a simple sentence on the wall.
The sentence was this: If you are not yet at ease
with your father and mother, then go away. I cannot help you.
Why? Because the problem has arisen there
and it has to be solved there.
That's why all the old Eastern traditions say
love your father, respect your father
as deeply as possible, because the ego arises there,
that is the soil. Solve it there,
otherwise it will haunt you everywhere.

Now psycho-analysts have also stumbled upon the fact;
all that psycho-analysis does is it brings you back
to the problems that existed between you and your parents
and tries to solve them somehow.
If you can solve your conflict with your parents,
many other conflicts will simply disappear
because they are based on the basic conflict.
For example, a man who is not at ease with his father
cannot believe in God, because God is a father-figure—
the father of the whole.
A man who is not at ease with his father
cannot be at ease with the boss in the office—
never, because he is the father-figure.
A man who is not at ease with his father cannot be at ease
with his master or guru, because he is a father-figure.
That small conflict with your parents
continues to be reflected in all your relationships.

If you are not at ease with your mother,
you cannot be at ease with your wife
because she will be the representative woman;
and you cannot be at ease with women as such,
because your mother is the first woman,
she is the first model of a woman.
If you hate your mother,
or, if you have a certain conflict in your mind,
if you cannot be with your mother for a long time,
you feel bored and you want to escape,
you will not feel at ease with any woman in the world.
Because wherever a woman is, your mother is,
and a subtle relationship continues.

In India, in the ancient days, in the days of Upanishads,
whenever a newly married couple came to an enlightened man
the enlightened man would bless them with the blessing
that they would become father and mother of ten children.
And to the woman he would say: Let it be remembered
that unless your husband becomes your eleventh child
the marriage is not complete.

Why? Why should the husband become the eleventh child—
otherwise the marriage is not complete?
This is the reason:
if the man has come to terms with his mother,
he will finally find the mother again in his wife.
A man remains a child, and a woman is a born mother.
So the ultimate flowering of a woman
is to become a mother of the whole.
That's why I call my *sannyasins* 'Ma'—mothers.
And the ultimate peak of a man is to become child-like,
innocent again like a child,
then the whole world and existence becomes the mother.
This is the intrinsic potentiality—
but one has to come to terms with the father and mother.

Ego is born there, it has to be tackled there.
Otherwise you will go on cutting branches and leaves
and the root remains untouched.
If you have settled with your father and mother,
you have become mature. Now there is no ego.
Now you understand that you were helpless,

now you understand that you depended,
that you were not the centre of the world.
In fact, you were completely dependent:
you could not have survived.
Understanding this, the ego by and by fades,
and, once you are not in conflict with life,
you become loose and natural, you relax.
Then you float.
Then the world is not filled with enemies,
it is a family, an organic unity;
and the world is not against you, you can float with it.
That is the meaning of this small parable.

This is a parable used by Zen people and Taoists,
and I must tell you a few things before I enter into it.
Taoists and Zen people have always joked about Confucius.
This is, in fact, a joke.
Because Confucius, to them, is the pinnacle of the legal mind.
Confucius is the very paragon of ego—
subtle, polished, cultured.

The whole Confucian philosophy is
how to polish your ego in such a way that you retain it
without being in conflict with others.
That's what a cultured man is.
A cultured man is not humble, no never;
a cultured man is a very subtle egoist.
He is very cunning, clever.
He will not bring his ego into any relationship,
he will hide it, and he will try to show that he is very humble.
He will smile and bow down,
and you can see well that this is just diplomatic.
To live in the world, Confucius says,
you have to exist with other egos
and you should be very, very intelligent about how you behave,
otherwise unnecessary troubles are created.
So Confucius has three thousand three hundred rules
for how a man should behave.
For each step he has rules: how one should dress....

And try to see the difference
between the Taoist, Zen and Confucian minds.

Because that is how, all over the world,
the distinction has existed:
the moralist is different from the religious man.
The difference is very subtle.
A moralist tries to be humble; a religious man is humble.
A moralist poses humility all around—
it is a pose, it is a gesture, cultivated.

A religious person is simply humble, it is not a pose.
Finding that the ego is nonsense,
finding that the ego has no grounds to exist,
finding that the ego is just a childish dream,
misconceived in ignorance,
the religious man simply becomes egoless.
Finding no ground for the ego, the ego evaporates.
Not that he becomes humble, no, he simply becomes egoless.
How can he become humble when there is no ego?
Only ego can become humble, so who will become humble?
He simply comes to know that he is not,
that he is just a part of this vast organic universe.
He is not separate, so who is going to be an egoist
and who is going to be humble? He is not.
He simply finds there is nothing like a centre in him:
the centre is in the universe and he is part of it.
Religious people have said that if there is a God,
only he can be permitted to use the word 'I'.
Nobody else should use the word 'I'
because there is only one centre in existence.
There cannot be millions of centres,
because there are not millions of universes, only one universe.
So, if there is a centre, there can be only one centre.
We all participate in it,
but we cannot claim that centre in ourselves.
That's why Zen says: Don't be humble, be a no-self.

Because humility is a trick of the ego,
it is the polished ego, not vulgar.

So there are two types of ego.
The vulgar ego you will find
in the uncultured, uncivilised, uneducated person.
Then there is a cultured ego,
refined, polished, perfumed, very subtle;
you cannot detect it. Always posing humility,

humbleness, simplicity—these are all postures.
Confucius is the paragon of the civilised man,
he believes in civilisation, and he says that rules
have to be followed, strict discipline has to be imposed,
because life is a struggle.

And don't provoke anybody unnecessarily.
Conserve your energy, because you will need it in some fight.
So don't go on fighting with everybody,
because that is unnecessary. Conserve energy.
Then when there is really a need you can fight,
but that fight should be very cultivated and cultured.
How to sit and how to stand, how to move, how to behave—
Confucius has rules for them,
because there are millions of egos
and you have to find your path
through this vast jungle of egos.
And, if you want to reach the goal,
don't be unnecessarily in conflict with each and everybody.
Just passing, pass in such a humble way
that nobody hinders you.
So tnis humility is diplomacy; it is political, not religious.

Confucius is not a religious man at all.
Because of Confucius,
China could fall a victim to communism,
because Confucius has remained the central force in China.
Many people ask me how it happened
that such a religious country like China
could fall a victim to communism,
to an absolutely materialistic philosophy.
It is not an accident.
Buddha entered China with his teaching;
Lao Tzu lived there; Chuang Tzu lived there—
but they could never become the central force.
The central force has remained Confucius,
and Confucius and Marx are fellow-travellers
so there is no problem.
It is difficult for India to become communist.
It was very, very easy for China to become communist—
and so suddenly, and so easily,
because the Confucian trend
is absolutely political, diplomatic, material.

The Cataract at Luliang

Zen and Taoists have always laughed about Confucius,
and this is one of their subtle jokes. Try to understand it.

Confucius was looking at the cataract at Luliang.
It falls from a height of two hundred feet,
and its foam reaches fifteen miles away.
No scaly finny creature could survive therein.
Yet Confucius saw an old man go in.
Thinking the old man was suffering from some trouble
and was therefore desirous of ending his life,
Confucius bade a disciple run along the bank
to try to save him.

The old man emerged about a hundred paces off,
and with flowing hair, he went caroling along the bank.
Confucius followed him, and when he caught up with him he said:
I had thought, sir, you were a spirit.
but now I see you are a man. Kindly tell me,
is there any way to deal thus with the water?

It looked almost impossible to Confucius,
that in this big waterfall,
with the river falling from the height of two hundred feet,
and creating so much foam that it spread over fifteen miles,
an old man was going to take his bath, to bathe in the river.
It was impossible! The tremendous energy of the waterfall
would kill the man, he would not be able to come out again.
He would be forced into the river, to the rocks,
to the very bottom.
At first he thought that this man
must be going to commit suicide,
because you could not come alive out of this waterfall.
So he told a disciple to go by the bank and try to save him.
But the man jumped, and then a few paces away
he came out of the river, perfectly alive.
It was unbelievable!

Why? For Confucius it was unbelievable,
because he believed in fight.
He did not know how to flow with nature.
That is the joke in it. He did not know.
He might have known

all the rules and regulations and how to swim,
but he did not know how to flow with the river.
He did not know surrender, the secret of it.
So he couldn't believe his eyes.
He thought that this man must be a spirit:
the physical body cannot survive, it is against all rules.
He ran after the man and when he got hold of him, he asked:
*I had thought, sir, you were a spirit,
but now I see you are a man. Kindly tell me,
is there any way to deal thus with the water?*
You have done a miracle: it is unbelievable.
Is there a certain way to deal thus with the water?

Confucius believes always
in ways, methods, techniques—the way.
This is how the ego believes.

There are people who come to me and they say:
How to fall in love? Is there a way?
How to fall in love?
They ask for a way, a method, a certain technique.
They don't understand what they are asking.

Falling in love means
that now there is no way, no technique, no method.
That's why it is called 'falling in';
you are no more the controller, you simply fall in.
That's why people who are very head-oriented
will say: Love is blind.
Love is the only eye, the only vision,
but they will say that love is blind, and they will think
that this man has gone mad. It looks mad to the reason,
because the reason is a great manipulator.
Anything in which the control is lost
looks dangerous to the reason.
So Confucius asked for the way:
How do you behave with the river?
How have you survived, sir?
There must be some technique.

This is the technique-oriented mind,
the mind that creates all technologies in the world.
But there is a world of human heart,
and there is a world of human being and consciousness

The Cataract at Luliang

where no technology is possible.
All technologies are possible with matter;
with consciousness no technologies are possible.
In fact no control is possible.
The very effort to control,
or to make a thing happen, is egoistic.

Confucius doesn't know that there is something like surrender.

If you have been a lover of rivers,
and if you have been swimming in rivers,
you will understand what that old man said.
I myself have loved rivers very much, and to fall
in a whirlpool is one of the most beautiful experiences.

In rivers, particularly when they are flooded, in the rains,
many whirlpools are created, very powerful and strong.
The water moves round and round like a screw.
If you are caught in it, you will be forced,
pulled towards the bottom, and the deeper you go,
the stronger the whirl becomes.
The natural tendency of the ego is to fight with it.
Of course, because it looks like death,
and the ego is very much afraid of death.
The ego tries to fight with the whirl,
and if you fight with the whirl in a flooded river,
or near a waterfall where many whirls exist, you are lost,
because the whirl is very strong, you cannot fight with it.
Violence won't do—
the more you fight with it, the weaker you become
because the whirl goes on pulling you, and you are fighting.
With each effort to fight you are losing energy.
Soon you will be tired and the whirl will suck you downwards.

And this is the phenomenon of the whirl:
on the surface the whirl is big;
the deeper you go, the smaller and smaller the whirl becomes—
stronger, but smaller.
And nearly at the bottom the whirl is so small
you can simply get out of it with no fight.
In fact the whirl itself throws you out, near the bottom.
But you have to wait for the bottom.
If you start fighting on the surface, you are done,
you cannot survive.

I have tried with many whirls;
the experience is lovely.

And it is exactly as it happens in deep meditation,
because there also you fight.
When your inner being yawns, and the abyss opens,
it is just like a whirl:
if you start fighting, you will be crushed.
You have to allow it, you simply move with it,
you don't fight.
You simply move with it; wherever it leads, you go.
You preserve your energy; not a single iota of energy is lost,
because you are not fighting, you are moving with the whirl.
You are enjoying the whole phenomenon,
as if you are on the wings of the whirl, flying.
Within a second you are pulled to the bottom
because it is such a tremendous force. It kills many people.
And, once near the bottom, you can simply slip out of it—
there is even no need to slip out of it, you will slip out
because it is so small it cannot contain you.

The same exactly happens in deep meditation.
You feel suffocated, you feel in the grip of something,
possessed, being pulled to some magnetic force.
You start fighting and resisting.
If you resist, only then will your energy be sucked.

Jesus says a very unbelievable thing,
and Christians have been at a loss as to how to interpret it
for these two thousand years;
and they have not been able to interpret it.
Jesus says: Resist not evil.
Even if it is evil, don't resist;
because, if you resist, the evil will win.
You are such a tiny energy—resist not.
In the very fight you will be defeated.
Don't fight, and nobody can defeat you.
Even if a very evil force, the devil, is there,
if you don't fight, he cannot defeat you.
If you start fighting, you are already defeated.
Fight, and the failure is absolutely certain;
don't fight, and there is no possibility of failing.
Because how can you fail if you don't fight?

The Cataract at Luliang

This is the art of judo and ju-jitsu: not to fight.
In Japan, they have developed a very subtle art of judo.
The man who is trained in judo cannot be defeated,
because he doesn't fight. Even if you hit him,
he absorbs the energy that you have thrown by your hitting.
He doesn't resist; he doesn't fight.
And within minutes even a very strong person
can be defeated by a very weak person if he knows judo.

You observe it many times happening all around.
Every day you see small children falling—the whole day.
They fall, and they get up, and they forget about it.
But if you fall like a small child,
you will always be in the hospital.
What happens when a child falls?
He simply falls; he doesn't resist.
He moves with the pull, with the gravitation.
He simply falls—like a pillow falling, no resistance.
When you fall, you resist. You first try not to fall.
All your fibres, all your bones, become tense and strained.
When strained bones and a strained nervous system
fall unwillingly, fighting, then many things are broken.
Not because of gravitation, but because of your resistance.
You sometimes see a drunkard falling on the street,
lying down in the gutter—nothing!
By the morning he is absolutely okay,
he goes to the office—and every night he falls.
He must know some trick that you don't know.
What does he know?
Simply this: he is so drunk that he cannot resist.
He cannot resist, he simply falls,
like a feather drops down, with no inner resistance or fight.
That's why in the morning he is absolutely okay again,
laughing and going to the office.
If you fall like a drunkard, you will immediately
have to be transported to the hospital,
many fractures would have happened.
Those fractures happen because of your fight.

In judo they train the person not to fight.
If somebody attacks you, you simply absorb the attack.
If he hits you on your head, you absorb.
When somebody is hitting you on your head,

a certain amount of energy has come to his hand.
If you fight, then two energies fight and are destroyed.
If you don't fight, you become receptive.
It is a very difficult art. It takes many years to learn
because the ego again and again comes in.
Once you have known the knack of it,
then you simply absorb the energy of the enemy.
And soon, just by throwing out his energy, he becomes weak,
and by and by you become stronger.
He is defeated by his own effort
and you win with no effort.

This is what the old man said.
No, replied the man, I have no way;
plunging in with the whirl...
—with the whirl, not against the whirl—
...plunging in with the whirl, I come out with the swirl.
I have no way. It is all done by the whirl and the swirl.
I don't come in, I move with it—
plunging in with the whirl, I come out with the swirl.
I accommodate myself to the water, not the water to me.

This is the solution to all human problems.
The ego is trying to accommodate the whole world to itself.
This is the trouble.
A man who has no ego accommodates himself to the world.
In fact, it is not good to say that he accommodates—
he simply finds that he is accommodated.

The ego tries to accommodate everything to it;
this is very childish, just like a child.
A child wants everything to be done, instantly;
whatsoever he desires should be done immediately.
If he desires the moon,
the moon should be produced immediately, right now.
He cannot even wait.
A child wants everything, everybody, to accommodate to him.
A child is a dictator, and whenever a child is born
into a family, he changes the whole atmosphere.
He makes everybody a servant, his dictatorship has no end—
and the ego is born in that childhood.
The ego is the most immature phenomenon:

it is childish, immature, not knowing what it is doing.

Who are you? Why should the whole accommodate to you?
You are just like a wave on the ocean
and you are trying to make the ocean accommodate to you.
Foolish. Patently foolish.
There is no need for the whole to accommodate to you.
It cannot be possible; it is not possible.
You can go on thinking about it, but you will be a failure.
Ego is always a failure, because the impossible is asked.
Napoleons, Hitlers, Alexanders—ask them.
In the end, they are great failures.
Rich people—ask them, in the end.
They have accumulated much,
but they feel a deep failure inside.
You can accumulate power in many ways,
but you will be a failure.
Ego can never be victorious.

Mulla Nasrudin was telling stories to his child.
I was also listening, and the child was insisting on more,
so he invented a story. He said:
There was one worm who was an early-rising worm.
He woke up in *brahamamuhurta,* early in the morning,
thinking that religious and moral teachers
have always said that early rising is beautiful.
But he was caught by an early-rising bird
who was also a believer in religious precepts:
that to rise early is good.
The child was very excited and he said:
What happened to the other worm?
You said that one worm was an early riser—and the other?
Mulla said: Yes, he was a late riser, very lazy.
But a child found him asleep and killed him.

The child was a little confused. He said:
But what is the motto of the story?
Said Nasrudin: Motto? You cannot win.

Whatsoever you do, early riser or not,
in the end everybody is killed.
This is absolutely true about the ego—you cannot win.
Whatsoever you do, be it virtuous or good,

if this virtue and goodness is based on the ego,
you cannot win, you have the very seed of defeat in you.
You can serve people, become a great servant of the society,
but if the ego is the base, you cannot win.
You may do millions of good things, but if the ego is there,
poison is there. It will poison everything you do.
Be poor, be rich; be religious, be irreligous;
theist, atheist; moral, immoral; criminal, a saint—
it doesn't matter. You can't win if the ego is there,
because the ego is the seed of failure.
And if the ego is not there you cannot be defeated,
because there is nobody to be defeated.
Your victory is absolute.
This is the secret-most teaching of Zen.

Be in accord with the whole, move with the whole,
with the river. Don't even swim.
People try to swim against the current,
and then they are defeated.
Don't even swim. Can't you float?
Can't you just allow the river to take you? Allow the river.
You just move with it—relax with the river of life
and let it move you.
It reaches the ocean, you need not bother.

The old man said:
I accommodate myself to the water, not the water to me.
This should become a constant remembrance;
a constant mindfulness of it will help you tremendously.
Whenever you feel that you are fighting, relax.
Whatsoever the case, you float, you don't fight,
and then the goal is certain.
In fact, then there is no goal in the future;
right now, this very moment, you have attained it—
flow with nature, loose and natural,
allow nature to take its own course,
don't force it in any way,
remain passive, not aggressive and violent.
Just like a small child going for a walk with his father—
wherever the father goes, the child is simply going with him,
happy, not knowing where he is going, why he is going.
Even if the father is going to kill the child
there is no problem for the child.

The Cataract at Luliang

There is a Christian story.
A man thought that he had been ordered by God to kill his son.
He was to take the son to the forest,
so the son was very excited.
Early in the morning they had to leave,
and the son was awake by midnight and he was saying:
Father, when are we going?

The father was troubled, because he was going to kill the son
in the forest and the son was so excited,
he didn't know what was going to happen.
But the man believed in the voice of God,
in his own Father the man believed.
And the child believed in *his* father: there was trust.

The father took the child, and the child was very happy.
He had never been taken to the forest.
Then the father started sharpening the sword
with which he was going to kill,
and the child was very excited and was helping.
The father was crying inside because he knew
that this child didn't know what was going to happen.
Then the child asked: What are you going to do with this?
The father said: You don't know. I am going to kill.
And the child laughed, he was enjoying, and he said: When?
He was ready. This is what 'floating-with' means.

The father took the sword
and the child was leaning in front of him, happy, smiling;
it was a game.

I don't know whether the story is true or not,
but it seems to be true, should be true,
it carries a deep meaning.

Just in the middle, a voice was heard:
Stop! You trusted me and that's enough.
And the child was saying: Why have you stopped?
Do it! It is a good play.
The child was in a playful mood.

When you trust life, you trust God,
because life is God and there is no other God.
When you trust and float with it, even death is transformed.
Then there is no death.

You never tried to exist separately
so how can you die?
The whole always lives: only individuals come and go.
Waves come and go: the ocean goes on and on and on.
If you don't believe in yourself as a separate wave, ego,
then how can you die?
You will live always and always in the whole.
You lived before, when you were not,
you are living right now, when you think you are,
and you will live again, when you will not be there.
The dream of your being separate is the ego,
and the ego creates conflict.
Through conflicts you dissipate and die.
Through conflict you are miserable.
Through conflict you lose all that was possible to you—
millions of blessings are possible for you.
Every moment the benediction is possible;
every moment the ecstasy is possible, but you miss.
You miss because you are a fighter.

The man said:
*I accommodate myself to the water, not the water to me.
And so I am able to deal with it after this fashion.*
But it is not a method, it is not a technique, not a way;
it is an understanding.

And remember, finally, either ego can exist, or understanding,
both cannot exist together.
If the ego exists, you have no understanding;
you are just an ignorant child
believing that you are the centre of the whole,
and, finding that it is not so, you are miserable.
Finding that you are not the centre, you create your hell.
Understanding means understanding the whole situation.
Simply looking at the whole phenomenon of your life,
inner and outer, ego disappears.
With understanding there exists no ego,
understanding is the path, the way.

Then you are in accord,
in harmony, in rhythm, in step with life.
Then suddenly you come to feel that
you plunge in with the whirl and you come out with the swirl.

The Cataract at Luliang

And this game is eternal—
plunging in with the whirl, coming out with the swirl—
this is the eternal game.
That's what Hindus have called the *leela*,
the great cosmic play.
You come sometimes as a wave, and then you disappear.
Then again you come as a wave, and you disappear.
And this goes on and on,
there is no beginning to it and no end to it.
The ego has a beginning, the ego has an end,
but you, without the ego, are beginningless, endless.
You are the very eternity,
but in the whole, in accord with the whole.
Against the whole, you are a nightmare to yourself.

So either there is ego or understanding. The choice is yours.
There is no need to be humble, just understanding.
And it is as if you have lighted a candle in a dark room—
suddenly the darkness is not there,
because light and darkness cannot exist together.
So, ego and understanding cannot exist together.

The 'Master of Silence'
25th February 1975

There was a monk who called himself 'The Master of Silence'.
Actually he was a fraud and had no genuine understanding.

To sell his humbug Zen he had two eloquent attendant monks
to answer questions for him—
but, as if to show his inscrutable silent Zen,
he himself never uttered a word.

One day, during the absence of his two attendants,
a pilgrim came to him and asked:
Master, what is the Buddha?

Not knowing what to do, or how to answer,
he looked desperately around in all directions
for his missing mouthpieces.

The pilgrim, apparently pleased and satisfied,
thanked the master, and set out again on his journey.

On the road the pilgrim met the two attendant monks
on their way home.
He began telling them enthusiastically
what an enlightened being this Master of Silence is.

He said: I asked him what Buddha is
and he immediately turned his face to the east and to the west,
implying that human beings are always looking for Buddha
here and there, but actually,
Buddha is not to be found in any such directions.
Oh, what an enlightened master he is,
and how profound his teaching!

When the attendant monks returned,
the Master of Silence scolded them thus:
Where have you been all this time?
A while ago I was embarrassed to death and almost ruined
by an inquisitive pilgrim.

Life is a mystery.
The more you understand it, the more mysterious it becomes.
The more you know, the less you feel that you know.
The more you become aware of the depth, the infinite depth,
the more it becomes almost impossible to say anything about it.
Hence silence.

A man who knows remains in such awe,
such infinite wonderment, that even breathing stops.
Standing before the mystery of life, one is lost completely.

But there are problems,
and the first problem with the mystery of life
is that there is always the possibility of frauds,
people who can deceive others, people who can cheat.
In the world of science that is not possible.
Science moves on a plain ground with infinite caution—
logical, rational. If you utter something nonsensical,
immediately you will be caught,
because whatsoever you say can be verified.
Science is objective, and any assertion, any statement,
can be verified in experiments in the laboratories.

With religion everything is inner, subjective, mysterious,
and the path is not on a plain. It is a hilly track.
There are many ups and many downs,
and the path moves like a spiral.
Again and again you come to the same place,
maybe a little higher.
And whatsoever you say cannot be verified,
there is no criterion of verification.
Because it is inner, no experiment can prove or disprove it;
because it is mysterious,
no logical argumentation can decide this way or that.
That's why science is one,
but there exist almost three thousand religions in the world.
You cannot prove any religion false. Neither can you prove
any other religion to be true and authentic.
That is not possible, because no empirical test is possible.

A Buddha says that there is no self inside.
How to prove this, or how to disprove this?
If somebody says, 'I have seen God,' and he sounds sincere,
what to do? He may be a deluded lunatic,
he may have seen a hallucination,
or he may really have seen the reality of existence.
But how to prove, or disprove?
He cannot share his experience with anybody, it is inner.
It is not like an object you can place in the middle
and everybody can watch it, and everybody can experiment
and dissect it. You have to take it in faith.
He may sound absolutely sincere, and may be deluded;
he may not be cheating you, trying to cheat you,
he may be himself deceived. He may be a very true person,

but he has seen a dream and thinks it is real—
sometimes dreams have the quality that they look more real
than the reality itself. Then dreams look like visions.
He has heard the voice of God,
and he is so filled with it, so thrilled. But what to do?
How to prove that he has not gone mad,
that he has not projected his own mind and idea?
There is no possibility.

If there is one genuine religious man,
there are ninety-nine others all around him.
A few of them are deluded: poor, simple fellows, good at heart,
not trying to harm anybody, but still they harm.
Then there are a few cheats, robbers, deceivers:
cunning, clever people who are knowingly doing harm.
But the harm pays. You cannot find
a better business in the world than religion.
You can promise, and there is no need to deliver the goods,
because the goods are invisible.

I have heard an anecdote—in America
they invented invisible hair-pins for ladies.
One lady was purchasing them at a supermarket
and the salesman gave her a packet of invisible hair-pins.
She looked in the box and she couldn't see any.
Of course, they were invisible, so how can you see?
And she said: But I don't see anything in it.
The man said: They are invisible, so how can you see?
So the lady asked: Really? Are they invisible?
The man said: You are asking me? For seven days
we have been out of stock, and still we are selling them.
They are absolutely invisible.

When things are invisible, you can go on selling, promising.
There is no need to deliver the goods,
because in the first place they are invisible,
so nobody can ever detect them.
And you cannot find a better business than religion,
because the goods are invisible.
I have seen many people being deceived, many people deceiving.
And the thing is so subtle
that nothing can be said for or against.

For example, I know a man
who is a simple, plain, stupid man.
But stupidity has its own qualities.
Particularly in religion,
a stupid man can look like a *paramahansa*.
Because he is stupid, his behaviour is unexpected,
just like an enlightened man. The similarity is there.
Because he is stupid, he cannot utter
a single rational statement—just like an enlightened man.
He is foolish, he doesn't know what he is saying,
how he is behaving. Suddenly he can do anything;
and this sudden doing seems to be as if he belongs
to another world. He has epileptic fits,
but people think he is going into samadhi.
He needs electric shock treatment!
Suddenly he will go into a fit and swoon,
and the followers will beat their drums
and they will sing to the glory of God,
that their master has gone into great samadhi, ecstasy.
And his mouth starts foaming, and his saliva flows out—
he is simply in a fit. He has no intelligence.
But that is a quality, and there are deceivers around him
who go on spreading things about the 'baba'.

And many things happen near him: that is the miracle.
Many things happen, because many things happen
of their own accord. The baba is in a swoon,
and many people will feel their kundalini rising.
They are projecting.
There is a certain phenomenon: if you sit quietly
for a long period, the body accumulates energy,
and then the body starts moving, feeling restless.
Sudden jerks start coming—they think this is kundalini.
Kundalini is rising and when it rises in one person,
how can you lag behind?
Then others start.
Then it is just like if one person goes to the toilet,
then others feel the urge;
if one person sneezes, others have a tremendous sneeze
coming to them. It becomes infectious.
But, with so many things happening, the baba must be in samadhi.
He is simply in a fit.

The 'Master of Silence'

In the East it has been my observation
that only one genuine person exists, ninety-nine are false—
either themselves deceived, simple, poor people;
or deceivers, cunning, clever people.

This can go on, because the whole phenomenon is invisible.
What to do? How to judge? How to decide?
Religion is always dangerous. It is dangerous
because the very terrain is mysterious, irrational.
Anything goes, and there is no outer way to judge it.
And there are people with their gullible minds, always ready
to believe something, because they need some foothold.
Without belief they feel unanchored, uprooted;
they need somebody to believe in,
they need somewhere to go and feel anchored and rooted.

Belief is a deep need in people. Why is it a deep need?
Because without belief you feel like a chaos;
without belief you don't know why you exist;
without belief you cannot feel any meaning in life.
No significance seems to be there.
You feel like an accident with no reason at all to be here.
Without belief, the question arises: Why are you? Who are you?
From where are you coming? Where are you going?
And there is not a single answer—
without belief there is no answer.
One feels simply without any meaning, an accident in existence,
not needed at all, not indispensible.
You will die and nobody will bother; they will all continue.
You feel something is lacking, a contact with reality,
a certain belief. That's why religions exist—
to supply beliefs, because people need them.

A person without belief has to be very, very courageous.
To live without belief is to live in the unknown,
to live without belief is a great daring
Ordinary people cannot afford that.
With too much daring, anguish comes in, anxiety is created.
And this has to be noted:
to me a real religious person is without belief.
Trust he has, but not belief,
and there is a vast difference between the two.

Belief is intellectual. You need it, that's why you have it.
It is there because you cannot live without belief.
Belief gives you a support to live by;
it gives you a certain meaning, howsoever false;
it gives you a certain blueprint for life,
how to move, where to move.
You are on the highway, not lost in a forest.
Belief gives you a community,
there are other believers just like you;
you become part of a crowd.
Then you need not think on your own,
then you are no longer responsible for your own being
and what you are doing.
Now you throw the responsibility on the crowd.

An individual Hindu is never so bad as a Hindu crowd.
An individual Mohammedan is never so bad as a Mohammedan crowd.
What happens? Individuals are not bad, crowds are simply mad—
because, in a crowd, nobody feels responsible.
You can commit murders in a crowd easily,
because you know the crowd is doing it
and you are just a wave in it, you are not the deciding factor,
so you are not responsible.
Individual, alone, you feel a responsibility.
You will feel guilty if you commit something.
It is my observation that sin exists through crowds,
no individual is ever a sinner.
And individuals, even if they commit something wrong,
can be taken out of it very easily; but crowds are impossible,
because crowds have no souls, no centres. To whom to appeal?

And in all that goes on in the world
—the devil, the evil forces—
the crowd is in fact responsible.
Nations are the devil;
religious communities are the evil forces.
Belief makes you a part of a bigger crowd than you,
and there is a feeling of elation
when you are a part of something bigger, a nation—
India, or America, or England.
Then you are not a tiny human being.
A great energy comes to you and you feel elated.
A euphoria is felt. That's why, whenever a country is at war,

people feel very euphoric, ecstatic.
Suddenly their life has a meaning—
they exist for the country,
for the religion, for the civilisation;
now they have a certain goal to be achieved,
and a certain treasure to be protected.
Now they are no longer ordinary people,
they have a great mission.
Belief is the bridge from the individual to the crowd.

Trust is totally different.
Trust is not an intellectual concept.
Trust is a quality of the heart, not of the head.
Belief is a bridge between the individual and the crowd,
and trust is a bridge between the individual and the cosmos.
Trust is always in God, and when I say 'God',
I don't mean any belief in God.
When I say God, I simply mean the whole.

Trust is a deep understanding that you are simply a part,
a note in a great symphony, just a small wave in the ocean.
Trust means you have to follow the whole, flow with the whole,
be in accord with the whole. Trust means:
I am not here as an enemy, I am not here to fight;
I am here to enjoy the opportunity that has been given to me;
I am here to be grateful and celebrating.
Trust is not in a doctrine: you need not be a Hindu,
you need not be a Mohammedan, you need not be a Jain or a Sikh.
Trust is a commitment between the individual and the whole.
Trust makes you religious
—not Hindu, not Mohammedan, not Christian—
simply religious. Trust has no name.
Belief makes you a Hindu, Mohammedan, Christian.
Belief has names, millions of names;
there are thousands of beliefs—you can choose.
Trust has only one quality:
the quality of surrender into the whole;
the quality of moving in accord with the whole;
the quality of not forcing the whole to follow you,
but simply allowing yourself to move with the whole.
Trust is a transformation; trust has to be attained;
belief is given by birth.
Nobody is born in trust, everybody is born in belief:

you are born a Hindu, or a Jain, or a Buddhist.
Belief is given by society,
because belief is the bridge between you and society.

If society doesn't give you a belief, there is a fear—
you may become rebellious.
In fact it is certain
that if the belief is not given, you will become rebellious,
and society doesn't want that, can't afford that.
Society, before you become aware, gives you deep beliefs.
Into your blood it goes—with the milk of your mother
the poison of belief seeps into your being.
By the time you become aware of what has happened
you find you are already a Hindu,
or a Mohammedan, or a Christian.
The straitjacket is already there: you are imprisoned.

And it is very difficult to get out of it
because it gets into your unconscious,
it becomes your very foundation.
Even if you get out of it, even if you go against it,
it will remain in the foundation,
because to cleanse the unconscious is very difficult.
Consciously you can't do it.

I have heard, it happened that Mulla Nasrudin
became an atheist. And he was dying, so the priest came.
The priest said: Mulla, now this is the last moment
and the last opportunity. Still there is time left,
you confess your sin and you confess
that you went wrong by becoming an atheist.
Become a theist and die believing in God.

Mulla Nasrudin opened his eyes and said:
Thank God I am not a theist.

Even if you are not a theist, you will thank God.
Deep down it remains in the unconscious,
it becomes a foundation.
Whatsoever you have learned in your childhood
before the age of seven, has become your foundation.
To uproot it, very great effort and meditation is needed.
You will have to move back, only then can it be wiped out.

You can create anti-beliefs, they won't help, they cannot help.
You can become a theist.
You can be a Hindu in your childhood,
then you can be converted to a Christian,
but you will remain a Hindu—
your Christianity will be coloured by your Hinduism.
You may become a communist, but, deep down,
the unconscious is there and it will colour your communism.
A deep meditation is needed to cleanse the unconscious.

Trust is totally different.
Trust is not in words, in scriptures. Trust is towards life—
the very energy that moves the whole.
You trust it and you float with it.
If it takes you down in the whirl, you go down in the whirl.
If it takes you out in the swirl, you come out in the swirl.
You move with it, you don't have your own mind about it.
If it makes you sad, you become sad.
If it makes you happy, you become happy.
You simply move with it, with no mind of your own,
and suddenly, you come to realise
that now you have achieved a point
where bliss is going to be eternal.
In your sadness also you will be blissful,
because it is none of your business.
The whole is doing it that way and you are moving with it.
Happiness—okay. Sadness—okay. You simply 'okay'.
Everything is okayed.
This is what a religious man is: he has no mind of his own.
Belief has a very strong mind of its own.

It is said about a great saint, Tulsidas,
that he was invited into a Krishna temple in Mathura,
and he was a believer in Ram.
He went there, but he would not bow down,
because the statue was of Krishna with a flute on his lips.
It is said that he said to Krishna: I can bow down only to Ram,
so, if you want me to bow down,
you take the bow of Ram in your hand.
When I see that you have become Ram, only then will I bow down.

This is the mind of belief.

Otherwise, what is the distinction between Ram and Krishna?
And what is the distinction between a flute and a bow?

And the story goes on: it says that the statue changed,
it became the statue of Ram,
and then Tulsidas bowed down very happily.

Now the problem is, what must have happened?
My understanding is that the statue
must have remained the same, because statues don't bother.
They don't bother whether you bow down or not.
But the mind of a believer can create things.
Tulsidas must have projected;
it must have been a projection,
it must have been a hallucination.
He must have seen, that's certain.
He must have seen, otherwise he would not have bowed down:
that's certain. The possibility is that his own mind created,
and when you are too filled with belief you can create.
You can see things which are not there,
and you can miss things which are there.
A mind that is filled with belief
is a mind which can project anything according to the belief.
When you see things, always remember this.

People come to me....
If somebody is a believer in Krishna and he meditates,
immediately Krishna starts coming to him.
Visions. But Christ never comes to him.
A Christian starts meditation—
then Krishna never disturbs his meditation, only Christ comes.
To a Mohammedan, neither Krishna nor Christ comes;
and Mohammed cannot come
because Mohammedans have no pictures of Mohammed.
They don't know what he looked like, so they cannot project.

Whatsoever you believe, you project. Belief is a projection.
It is just like a projector in a movie film-house:
you see something on the screen which is not there.
The projector is hidden behind,
but you never look at the projector, you look at the screen.
The projector is at the back,
and the whole game is going on there,
but you look at the screen.

The whole game is going on in your mind,
and a mind filled with belief
always goes on projecting things in the world,
it sees things which are not there.
This is the problem.
The mind which believes is always vulnerable
and always provides an opportunity to be exploited
by the cheaters—and the cheaters are all around.
The whole path is filled with robbers, because no map exists.

Moving into religion is moving into the uncharted,
into the unmapped. Robbers can flourish there very easily,
they can wait for you—and they are waiting.
And sometimes, even if the person is not deceiving you,
you want to be deceived. Then you will be deceived.
Nobody can deceive you if, deep down,
you are not ready to be deceived.

Just a few days before, a man came to me and he said:
A baba has deceived me, and he is a great yogi.
I asked him: And what has he done?
He said: He can make gold out of any metal.
He has shown me and I have seen it happening with my own eyes.
Then he said that I should bring all my gold
and he would make it tenfold.
So I collected all my ornaments
and he has simply escaped with them. He has deceived me.

Everybody will think that he had deceived him,
but I told this man: It is your greed that has deceived you.
Don't throw the responsibility onto anybody else.
You are simply foolish. Greed is foolish.
You wanted your ornaments to be made tenfold.
That mind has deceived you,
the other person has simply used the opportunity.
He is just a clever person, that's all.
You are the real problem.
If he had not deceived you, somebody else would have.

So who deceives is not the question.
It has been my observation that if somebody deceives you,
it shows a certain proneness in you to be deceived.
And if somebody can lie to you,

it means you have a certain affinity with lies.
A man of truth cannot be deceived.
A man who lives in truth cannot become a victim of liars.
Only a liar can be deceived by another liar;
otherwise there is no possibility.
There are millions of people who are ready to be deceived,
who are simply waiting for someone to come
and deceive them—because of their beliefs,
because of their vicious desires, because of their greed.
And remember well that greed is greed,
whether it exists in the material world or in the spiritual
makes no difference. The quality of it remains the same.
You would like somebody to increase your gold tenfold—
this is greed.
Then somebody says, 'I will make you an enlightened person,'
and you fall in line immediately. That too is greed.

And I tell you: It is possible
to increase gold tenfold very easily,
but it is almost impossible to make any other person enlightened.
Because that is no game. The path is arduous.
In fact nobody ever makes you enlightened—
you yourself become enlightened;
the other may be a catalytic agent at the most, nothing more.
But in fact everything happens within you;
the other's presence may have helped, that's all.
And if you are really sincere, even that is not needed.
If you are sincere, those who can help will seek you,
if you are insincere, you will seek those who can harm.
That is the difference. When a disciple seeks a master,
there is almost always going to be something wrong.
When a master seeks a disciple,
only then something authentic is going to happen.

How can you seek the master?
Whatsoever you may think will be your mind,
and you are completely ignorant, you are a sleepwalker.
You will seek somebody according to you.
You will be the criterion.
Then you will go and seek somebody who is doing a miracle.

You may go and seek Satya Sai Baba,
because that will be a deep fulfillment of your greed.

The 'Master of Silence' 141

You will see: here is the man.
If he can produce things out of air, he can do anything.
Now your greed is provoked.
Now a deep affinity happens immediately.
That's why you will see
thousands of people around Satya Sai Baba.
If a Buddha exists, you will not see multitudes there,
because there is no affinity.
Satya Sai Baba has an appeal deep inside you:
your greed is provoked. Now you know this is the right man.
But you are wrong. How can you decide who is the right man?
You create your deceivers, you give them the opportunity.
You follow magicians, not masters.

If you really want to seek a master,
drop greed and drop your beliefs.
Go to a master completely nude in the mind, with no beliefs;
as if you are a tree in the fall with no leaves,
naked, standing against the sky.
You go and seek a master with a naked mind, with no leaves,
with no beliefs. Only then, only then, I say,
will you be able to see without projection;
only then will something penetrate into your life
from the above.
Then nobody can deceive you.

So don't be bothered and don't condemn the deceivers:
they fulfill a need. Because you need them, they are there.
Nothing exists without any cause.
People exist all around you, because you need them.
Thieves exist, robbers exist, exploiters exist,
deceivers exist, because you need them.
You will be nowhere if they all disappear;
you will be simply unable to live your life
if they are not there.

This story is beautiful, and has to be understood deeply.

There was a monk who called himself 'The Master of Silence'.
Actually he was a fraud and had no genuine understanding.

You can pretend, and in religion
you can pretend more than anywhere else.

Because people are clever in their worldly ways
but they are completely innocent
as far as religion is concerned.
You may be able to know everything
that goes on in the market, you have lived there,
you know the tricks and the ways and everything—
you have yourself been doing those things.
You are wise as far as the world is concerned,
but when you move into the world of a monastery,
from the market to the monastery, there is a great difference.
In the monastery you are completely innocent, like a child.
You may be very old, sixty or seventy years of age,
but in a monastery, in a temple,
you are just like a small child. You have not lived there,
and the same things exist there also. Again it is a market.

When Jesus entered the temple of Jerusalem,
he entered with a whip and he started beating people,
because many shopkeepers had entered the temple
and many money-lenders. He turned their tables upside down
and he said: You have made my God's temple a market.
You traders—you get out!
This is really something—one single man,
and the whole crowd of traders escaped.

Truth has a strength of its own.
When something is true, you immediately become weak,
because you are a liar and you immediately understand:
That's right.
Those shopkeepers didn't fight;
those money-lenders could have killed Jesus;
he was alone and they were many.
But simply at the truth of it they escaped outside.
And only when they reached outside
did they start planning what to do with this man—
and it was their planning that finally crucified Jesus.

In the monasteries, in the temples, in the ashrams,
another world exists.
You don't know the laws of it, the rules of the game.
You can be deceived there very, very easily.
And pretenders abound, because it is so easy.

This has been my feeling:

The 'Master of Silence'

two types of people move towards religion.
One is the man who has lived in the world,
lived it through and through, and has come to understand
that it is futile, useless, a wastage of life.
It is just like a dream,
and that too not a beautiful dream, but a nightmare.
This is one type, the genuine type, the authentic,
who has lived through the world and found it useless,
a desert, with no oasis in it, and has turned away.
His turning is total. He will not look back.
There is nothing to look back to.
Buddha used to ask his disciples:
Have you really turned completely
or would you like to have a little of your mind
always looking back, a part of you always looking back?
This is the first type who is really genuine,
who has lived in the world and found it just a frustration.
That's why he has moved towards religion.

Then there is another type which is completely opposite.
The first type is one per cent,
the second type is ninety-nine per cent.
These people are very much attracted towards religion.
This type are those people who couldn't succeed in the world,
who couldn't succeed in their ambitions,
who could not become important.
They would have liked to have become prime ministers
and presidents, but they couldn't.
They were simply not made that strong to fight there.
They are people who would have like to have
become Rockefellers, or Fords,
but could not because the competition was too great
and they were not made of the right strong metal.
They were lacking, because life is a struggle
and they were simply inferior.
They didn't have that much intelligence,
or that kind of strength to fight through
and to fulfill their ambitions.
These people also turn towards religion.

These are the great deceivers.
They will become the problem for religion
and for people who seek religion.

They will be the deceivers all around the temple;
they will make the temple a trade-house
because their desires are still there lurking.
They have turned to religion as politicians—
of course, politicians who have failed in politics.
You go all over the country—around gurus everywhere
you will find politicians who have failed.
Ex-ministers will always be found coming to some guru—
people who wanted too much in the world and couldn't get it,
they turn towards religion, because there things are easier.
Competition is not much, and you can pretend,
and you can believe easily that you are a very superior being.
And there is no competition.
You can simply say, 'I have become enlightened,'
and nobody can deny it, and nobody can disprove it.
There simply exists no criterion to judge it,
and you can always find foolish people to follow you.

Even a Muktanand can get followers.
Once I passed Muktanand's ashram,
and just to see what was happening there, I went in.
I have never seen such an ordinary man
becoming a great religious leader of people.
No potential, no achievement, no insight—
if you saw him walking in the street
you would not recognize that there is something there.
Just plain ordinary—and not ordinary in the sense of Zen—
just plain ordinary. But even he can find followers.

In the world, millions of fools exist;
and they are always ready to believe, always ready,
ready to fall into the trap of anybody.
In fact, sometimes there is no trap at all, but they fall,
because they would like to believe that something is happening.
Man is so imaginative, and, because of his imagination,
he starts believing that something is happening.
These people know at least this much about what to do.

Somebody comes to me and says:
I have a certain pain in my backbone.
Now, if I say that this is simply a pain, go to a doctor,
he simply turns away from me and never comes back,
because he had not come for that. He had come for an approval.

The 'Master of Silence'

If I say: Yes, your kundalini is rising, he will be happy.
These fools will always find their Muktanands.

And not very ordinary people,
sometimes very intelligent people come.
Just a few days before, a film producer came to me—
a very well-known name all over India.
His blood sugar has gone beyond all ordinary limits;
it has reached five hundred. He should really be dead by now.
He is a drunkard, and a great food eater,
obsessed with eating, but still he continues and continues
eating sweets and drinking alcohol.
Now, because of so much blood sugar,
his whole body is trembling. It has to,
because his whole body is ill, every fibre of it is ill,
and there is a deep trembling inside.
He was sitting there when I was talking to others,
and he was trembling. Then he asked me:
What do you think? What is it—is it kundalini rising?

Now what to do with these people? These are the victims,
and these are participants in creating deceivers;
they are also half responsible.
And I know this man also belongs to Muktanand's group.

Now the problem arises for me—what to do?
If I say: 'Yes. It is Kundalini rising and this is
your last life. Soon, within days, you will be enlightened,'
he will bow down, touch my feet and will go away very happy.
He will be happy, I will be happy, and everything is settled.
And he will go around talking about me,
that this is the right, the greatest master
that he has come to know. It is a good business. Simple.
But then I am deceiving him, and not only deceiving,
I am killing him, I am a murderer,
because I know that he is dying of diabetes,
and the diabetes has gone beyond all limits.
If I say, 'This is kundalini and enlightenment is coming,
and this is like samadhi, that's why you are trembling;
it is God descending into you,'
or, 'You are rising towards the Divine,'
or, 'The Divine is descending in you,'
he will be very happy, everybody is happy, there is no problem.

He will work for me
and until he dies he will go on talking about me.

But the moment I said:
'This is nothing to do with any enlightenment.
This is simple—too much sugar in the blood.
Your whole body is feverish. You don't waste time,
you go to the doctors and listen to them,'
immediately I could see the change in his face. It changed:
This man is not a master at all. How can he be a master,
and enlightened, when he cannot understand
such a simple phenomenon that is happening in me?

It actually happened. A man, very well-known in the West,
Franklin Jones, was a disciple of Muktanand—
and then his kundalini arose.
Muktanand approved: You have become a *siddha*.
Not only did he approve, he gave a written certificate.
I simply cannot believe what foolishnesses go on—
a certificate that you have become a *siddha*, enlightened!
So of course the man became a *siddha* and he changed his name.
He was Franklin Jones, now he is Bubba Free John,
and he has many followers of his own.

Now the trouble came in, because he had become more enlightened
than Muktanand ever expected,
and he had become a guru in his own right.
Now he wanted—he came again just a few months ago—
now he wanted another certificate.
Now he wanted to show:
There is no need for me to belong to any master,
because now I am a master myself,
and my karmas with you, with Muktanand, are fulfilled.
So, give me a certificate that I am absoutely free.

Now Muktanand hesitated—this was going too far.
So he denied, he would not give another certificate.
But the thing had already gone too far.
The man returned home, wrote a book, and said:
Of course Muktanand helped me a little on my way,
but he is not an enlightened man
and I dissolve all my links with him. He is an ordinary man.

This is how things go.

The 'Master of Silence'

He was an enlightened man because he gave the certificate,
he was the greatest master in the world. Now he is no longer.
He is an ordinary man—'I dissolve all my links with him.'

These things go on. Remember this,
because you can become a part in such a game yourself.
Never believe in yourself too much. Remain aware.
When you come to me I will say exactly what is happening.
Many have gone from me
because I will not support their egos
and I will not fulfill their wishes,
and I will not say what they want me to say.
And once they go away, they are against me,
they have to be. These are the traps.
Not only do the deceivers create them,
you help to create them.
Don't be a participant in any deception, be very, very alert.

This monk, who was a fraud and had no genuine understanding,
called himself 'The Master of Silence'.
That's very beautiful,
because if you utter something you can be caught.
It is simply beautiful to remain silent;
then nobody can catch you.
They say it is good for two kinds of persons to be silent:
the very, very wise have to be silent,
because what they know cannot be said;
and the very, very foolish,
because if they are not silent, they will be caught.
So this man, who was a fraud, used to call himself
'The Master of Silence'. He would not utter a single word.
But if you don't utter a word you cannot sell anything.
If a salesman is silent, how will he sell things?
So he devised a plan.

*To sell his humbug Zen he had two eloquent attendant monks
to answer questions for him—
but, as if to show his inscrutable silent Zen,
he himself never uttered a word.*

*One day, during the absence of his two attendants,
a pilgrim came to him and asked:*

Master, what is the Buddha?

This is one of the Zen questions.
It means: what is *dharma,* what is religion?
It means: what is awareness?
It means: what is an awakened being?
It is one of the most fundamental questions in Zen—
What is the Buddha?
What is that utterly enlightened state of being
that we call Buddha?

*Not knowing what to do, or how to answer,
he looked desperately around in all directions
for his missing mouthpieces.*

*The pilgrim, apparently pleased and satisfied,
thanked the master and set out again on his journey.*

*On the road the pilgrim met the two attendant monks
on their way home.
He began telling them enthusiastically
what an enlightened being this Master of Silence is.*

He projected, of course.
He must have heard that those who know remain silent.
He must have read it in the scriptures
where it is said millions of times
that one who knows, never says; one who says, has not known yet.

But these are very, very paradoxical things.
Lao Tzu says, in the very beginning of 'Tao-Te-Ching',
that truth cannot be uttered,
and that which can be uttered is not true.
But Lao Tzu uttered this—so what to think about it?
Is it true, or not?
It is the uttered word, it has been said.
Now you will be in very deep trouble. Lao Tzu says
that truth cannot be said, but this much he is saying.
So is this saying true or not?
If it is not true that will mean that truth can be uttered;
if it is true then even this cannot be uttered.

Religion is full of paradoxes and that's the problem.
This man must have read many Zen masters

The 'Master of Silence'

saying that truth cannot be said.
This is right: truth cannot be said.
But this much can be said, many things can be said,
millions of things can be said which will be helpful
to find that which cannot be said.
Many things can be indicated,
and that which cannot be said can at least be shown.
The whole meaning is only this:
that the truth is greater than the words.
It is greater than the silence also.
Truth is so vast
that it cannot be forced into the capsule of words
and it cannot be forced into silence either.
In fact, silence exists in truth,
and words also exist in truth.
Truth is the very sky, the very space.

This master pulled a trick.
Thinking that truth cannot be said,
the best way is to keep silent—
but then no one will be attracted to you.
So he had two attendants to talk about him—mouthpieces.
That is a good arrangement,
because if they say something wrong, he is not involved,
if they say something right—so far, so good.
But one day he was caught.
You can deceive people for the time-being,
but you cannot deceive people for ever.
Some day, somewhere, you will be caught.
You cannot make an arrangement of lies
which can go on for ever and for ever. The truth will erupt.
Ninety-nine per cent of the time you may succeed,
but one per cent you will fail.
And that one per cent will bring the whole success to failure.
It will destroy the whole thing.

One day a pilgrim came and asked: What is the Buddha?
The master desperately looked this way and that
in all directions for his missing mouthpieces.
This was the truth, he had no answer to give.
And by looking in all directions, he was looking
for something else—not for truth, not for Buddha,

not to indicate anything by a gesture.
But the pilgrim projected.
By his looking in all directions, the pilgrim thought
that he was really a Zen master, a great master.
He would not utter words, but he was showing
that you can look in every dimension, in every direction,
and you will not find Buddha there, because Buddha is inside.
You can seek and search and you will not find,
because he is in the seeker himself.
This was the projection, and this is what you can do easily.
This is how people are deceived—
they have their own minds and beliefs and concepts and theories,
and they project.

Many times it has happened to me. People project.
A man came. He came with a bag.
I didn't know what he had in the bag.
He touched my feet and the bag was in his hand,
so the bag also touched my feet.
I thought it was just accidental.
But the man had a bottle with water in it inside the bag,
and it was not accidental.
He wanted my feet to touch the bottle,
and I was completely unaware of what he was doing.
Then, after a few days, he came and he thanked me,
and he was very, very grateful.
He said: You cured my illness.
I asked: What illness? I don't know your illness.
He said: I had a severe headache for many years,
a sort of migraine, and the water I brought last time I came,
you touched it with your feet.
I said: I never touched it with my feet.
He said: Whatsoever is the case, you touched the bottle
and I drank it for a few days
and the headache is completely gone.

Now what to do?
If I say that this is simply his own magic, he has done it,
it is an auto-hypnosis, then there is a possibility
that the headache may come back;
because you cannot believe in yourself,
you are always believing somebody.
You cannot believe in yourself—

The 'Master of Silence'

but if you cannot believe in yourself,
how can you believe in anybody?
But this goes on.
You feel impotent inside: you cannot believe in yourself.
You seek somebody, and through somebody's belief,
your own magic, your own auto-hypnosis starts working.
This man was cured. In the first place,
his headache must have been created by himself
—because a real headache cannot be cured in such a way,
only a false headache, a psychological one—
in the first place the headache was a hypnosis;
in the second place, he had cured it.
But this man is dangerous,
because if you can create a headache
you can also create cancer.
Projecting things....

Once it happened that a man stayed with me
and we were sleeping in the same room.
In the night I must have gone to the toilet
and he must have been very sleepy, half awake, half asleep.
So he looked at my bed and I was not there.
Then he must have fallen asleep for a few seconds.
When I came back and he must have looked again—I was there!
So he thought that for those few seconds I had disappeared.
He jumped out of the bed, caught my legs and said:
Just tell me—you have done the miracle—
but tell me how you did it?
Now I will never leave you. You are the right master!
So I told him: It is okay. You will not leave me;
but at least give me a chance also
to say whether I would like you to be with me always, or not—
because you are simply a fool.
But the man said:
No, you don't try to escape. I am not going to leave you.
I have seen the miracle: for this I was waiting.
I will choose the master who can disappear.
You have done it. I have seen it with my own eyes!

Mind is a very subtle game.
You can hear things I am not saying;
you can go through things I am not doing;

you can deceive yourself.
So it is not necessary that somebody should deceive you.
You can deceive yourself.
You are a self-deceiver.

The man, seeing the silent master looking desperately all around,
thought that this was the right man, a great enlightened man,
indicating that the Buddha cannot be found anywhere.
So, satisfied, well pleased, he thanked the master
and set out again on his journey.
*On the road the pilgrim met the attendant monks
on their way home.
He began telling them enthusiastically
what an enlightened being this Master of Silence is.*

*He said: I asked him what Buddha is
and he immediately turned his face to the east and to the west,
implying that human beings are always looking for Buddha
here and there, but actually,
Buddha is not to be found in any such directions.
Oh, what an enlightened master he is,
and how profound his teaching!*

*When the attendant monks returned,
the Master of Silence scolded them thus:
Where have you been all this time?
A while ago I was embarrassed to death and almost ruined
by an inquisitive pilgrim.*

Remember this story well,
because it can be your story also on the path.
And this should not be so—
this story should not become your story.
I am telling these stories and talking about them
to make you aware of certain things.
I love these stories, because they indicate so simply
and so directly and so immediately certain phenomena
which are possible for every pilgrim to meet on the path.
How to avoid them so that you are not deceived?
Nothing can be done about the deceivers. What can you do?
They are there and the whole allows them also—
that far it is good.

The 'Master of Silence'

You cannot do anything about the deceivers,
so don't be worried, let them be themselves.
But you can do something about yourself, that is the point.

I don't want you to become revolutionaries
and go and hunt babas. No. Leave them to themselves.
I'm telling you, not to become revolutionaries,
but to become more aware
so that such things don't happen to you, that's all.
Babas will continue, always and always,
because fools are there, and they need them;
they fulfill a particular need.

So what is to be done? You can do only one thing.
You drop that need within you. Don't project.
Don't allow beliefs to settle in your mind.
Clean the mind every day, as one cleans the house;
dust gathers the whole day, in the evening you clean it,
and again in the morning.
In the night you have done nothing, but even in the night
dust settles, so in the morning you clean again.
Continuously clean your mind of beliefs, concepts, theories,
ideas, ideologies, philosophies, doctrines, scriptures.
You simply clean your mind of verbal chattering
and you try to look at reality without any mind inside.
Just look, a pure look, stare naked.
Tilopa says: Stare naked and *mahamudra* will be yours.
You will attain to the highest enlightenment
possible to human consciousness. Stare naked.
Let your eyes be clean of all concepts.
Then the reality will be revealed to you,
because you will not distort it and you will not project it
and you will not put anything into it.

What did this pilgrim do? He had some ideas
and he put these ideas into the gesture of the master
who was looking all around for his mouthpieces.
Into that situation he put his own ideas.
He must have read somewhere that the Buddha
cannot be found in any direction. That was projected.

Don't be a projector, don't be an active mind.
Let your mind be completely passive, receptive.

Don't bring anything from the mind into the reality,
otherwise you will distort it.
Simply allow the reality to enter the mind
and you be a passive watcher, a passive witness.
Then, whatsoever the case is, you will know.
Then that which is will be revealed to you,
and only that can lead you to maturity, to growth,
and to the final flowering.

Drop the mind if you want to know the real.
Put aside the mind if you want to penetrate into the truth.
The truth is always there,
but your mind is standing just in-between.
Put aside the mind, make a window and look,
and everything, the very mystery of life,
becomes unveiled before you.
With the mind nobody has ever been able to know the truth.
Without the mind anybody can know the truth,
because the mind is the only barrier.
The mind must cease for the truth to be.

And you have nothing else but mind,
so it is difficult, very difficult to put it aside—arduous,
but it happens if you go on trying.
In the beginning only a few seconds of glimpses will be there.
But even those will give you a new dimension.
For seconds mind stops, and suddenly, as if there is lightning,
the whole world of mind disappears
and the world of the real is revealed.
These lightnings will happen to you, and then,
by and by, you will get settled into the state of no-mind.
Then there is no need for lightning, the sun has arisen.
Now it is the morning, all darkness disappears.

A religious person is a person of no mind, no belief.
A religious person is a person of trust.

Awakening
26th February 1975

During three years of severe training
under the great master Gizan,
Koshu was unable to gain satori.

At the beginning of a special seven-day session of discipline,
he thought his chance had finally come.
He climbed the tower of the temple gate,
and going up to the arhat images he made this vow:
Either I realise my dreams up here,
or they'll find my dead body at the foot of this tower.

He went without food or sleep, giving himself up
to constant za-zen, often crying out things like:
What was my karma that in spite of all these efforts
I can't grasp the way?

At last he admitted failure, and, determined to end it all,
he went to the railing and slowly lifted his leg over it.
At that very instant he had an awakening.

Overjoyed, he rushed down the stairs and through the rain
to Gizan's room.

Before he had a chance to speak, the master cried:
Bravo!—you've finally had your day.

Man is the only animal who can think of, try to,
or actually commit suicide.
Suicide is very special. It is human.

Animals live, they die, but they cannot commit suicide.
They live, but there are not any problems,
life doesn't create any 'angst', anguish.
Life is not an anxiety for them—they simply live it;
and then, as simply as they live, they simply die.
Animals don't have any death consciousness.
In fact, they are neither aware of life, nor of death,
so the question of suicide doesn't arise.
They are not conscious at all;
they live in the deepest sleep of the unconscious.

Only man can commit suicide.
That means that only man can do something about life or death;
it means that only man can stand against life.
This possibility is there because man is conscious.
But remember, the problems of life, the anxiety, the tension,
the anguish, or the final decision to commit suicide,
do not come out of consciousness—
they come out of a fragmentary consciousness.

This has to be understood deeply.
A Buddha is also conscious, but he cannot commit suicide,
cannot even think about it.
Suicide doesn't exist for a Buddha,
but he is also conscious. Why?
Animals are unconscious totally; Buddha is conscious totally.
With total consciousness there is no problem,
or, with total unconsciousness there is no problem.
In fact, to be total in any way is to be beyond problems.

A man is fragmentarily conscious:
a part of him has become conscious.
That creates the whole problem.
The remaining, the greater part, remains unconscious.
Man has become two.
One part is conscious, the remaining whole is unconscious.
A discontinuity has happened in man.
He is not one whole. He is not one piece. He is double.
The duality has come in.
He is just like an iceberg, floating in the ocean:
one-tenth is out of the water,
nine-tenths is hidden underneath.
The same is the proportion
of human consciousness and unconsciousness:
one-tenth of consciousness has become conscious,
nine-tenths of consciousness is still in the unconscious.
Just the top layer is conscious, and the whole being
remains underneath in deep darkness.

Of course there are going to be problems,
because a conflict has arisen in the being.
You have become two; and the conscious part is so small
that it is almost impotent.
It can talk, it is very articulate; it can think;

but when the moment comes to do something,
it is the unconscious which is needed
because the unconscious has the energy to do it.
You can decide that you will not be angry again,
but this decision comes from the impotent part of the mind,
the part which is conscious;
which can see that anger is futile, harmful, poisonous;
which can see the whole situation, and decide.
But the decision has no power behind it, because all power
belongs to the whole which is still unconscious.
The conscious part decides, 'I will not be angry again,'
and it is not—until the situation arises.
When the situation arises, the conscious is pushed aside,
and the unconscious surfaces.
It is vital, it is forceful, it has energy,
and suddenly you are overpowered.
The conscious may try a little while, but it is useless—
against the tide it is nothing.
When the unconscious becomes a tide
and comes to take over a situation, you are possessed,
you are no more yourself as you know yourself to be,
your ego is thrown off-gear.

All the decisions taken by your conscious
are simply insignificant:
it is the unconscious which does things.
Again, when the situation has gone, the unconscious recedes
and the conscious comes back onto the throne.
The conscious comes on the throne
only when the unconscious is not there.

It is like a servant.
When the emperor is not there
the servant sits on the throne and orders.
Of course, nobody is there to listen to him, he is alone.
When the emperor comes
the servant simply has to leave the throne
and listen to the emperor.
The bigger part of you always remains the emperor,
the lesser part remains like a servant.

Then much conflict arises,
because the part that decides cannot act,
and the part that acts cannot decide.

The part that sees things can think about them,
but has no energy;
and the part that cannot see, is completely blind,
has all the energy.

In animals there are not two parts,
only the unconscious exists, and with no thinking, it acts.
There is no problem, because there is no inner conflict.
In a Buddha, also, the same happens from the other end:
the whole has become conscious.
This is the meaning of enlightenment, satori, samadhi.
You have again become one like an animal—one piece.
Now, whatsoever Buddha decides, automatically it happens,
because there is nobody against it, nobody unaware of it.
There is no other in the house.
Buddha lives alone in the house, so Buddha need not struggle.
He sees a situation, he decides and acts.
In fact, decision and action are not two in a Buddha—
decision is the act.
He simply sees that anger is useless, and anger disappears.
There is no effort to impose on it, force it.
A Buddha remains loose and natural. He can afford to.
You cannot afford to be loose and natural,
because the moment you are loose and natural
the unconscious comes in.
You have to go on controlling yourself,
and the more you control, the more artificial you become.

A civilised human being is a plastic flower.
He has no vitality, no energy—
and when there is no energy, there is no delight.
One of the greatest English poets, William Blake,
has a beautiful line about it, a very deep insight.
He says: Energy is delight. There is no other delight.
The very vitality, the very energy of being,
is delight, is bliss.
Only impotence is misery, weakness is misery.
And duality creates impotence.

And whatsoever small energy is left
after you are divided in two,
that too goes as a wastage in the inner conflict.
You are continuously fighting inside,

continuously suppressing something,
continuously trying to force something else.
Anger comes, and you would like to be non-angry;
greed comes, and you would like to be greed-less;
possession comes, and you would like to be non-possessive;
violence comes, and you would like to be non-violent;
there is cruelty, and you go on imposing compassion;
there is much turmoil,
and you would like to be serene and silent;
something goes on inside,
and you go on imposing something else on it,
continuous fight dissipates the remaining energy.
And this is going to be so, unless you become one again.

There are two ways to become one:
either fall back to the animal, or rise up to the Buddha.

Of course, falling back is easier.
Effort will not be needed, you can simply slip back.
It is downhill, no effort; and going up is difficult.
Hence millions of people choose the downhill way.
What is the downhill way
as far as consciousness is concerned?
Drugs, alcohol, sex, are the downhill way.

In a deep sexual act you again become an animal,
you are no more human. The gap is bridged.
In a deep sexual orgasm, the duality disappears,
the controller is no more there. In a deep sexual act,
your whole starts functioning as a whole.
Mind is no longer there, ego is no longer there,
the controller and the control are no longer there,
because the sexual act is non-voluntary.
Your will is not needed, your will is not required.
You are no more a will, the will is surrendered.
Suddenly you are back to the world,
the animal world, the natural world;
again you have entered into the Garden of Eden,
again you are Adam or Eve—no more a civilised human being.

That's why all societies condemn sex. They are afraid of it.
It is a back door to the Garden of Eden.
All civilisations are afraid of sex. The fear comes,

because once you know an uncontrolled existence
then you would not like control at all.
You can become a rebel,
you can throw all the rules and regulations to the winds,
you can throw Confucius to the dust.
Again you can become an animal;
and civilisation is afraid of it.
So, sex is allowed, because if it is not allowed
then too it will create trouble.
It is such a deep-rooted instinct in the very biology,
in the very physiology of you, in the very deeper chemistry,
that if it is not allowed, it will create perversion,
you may go mad.
So society allows it in mild, homeopathic doses.
That is the meaning of marriage—marriage is
a mild, homeopathic dose controlled in a certain way.
You are allowed a little window out of society,
but society still manages the outer control.
Marriage is love plus law—
that 'plus law' is the control around it.
If love is allowed without any law,
the fear is that man will fall again into an animal world.

And the fear seems to be true; the fear has meaning.
Man can fall through love, because man can rise through love.
Man can fall through it because the ladder
is always the same whether you go up or you go down.
Love can rise to such heights that Jesus can say: Love is God.
And love can fall to such depths
that society is constantly on watch,
the police are always around, the magistrate is sitting there.

Love is not a freedom.
Why, in love, can man fall so deep?
Because in love the control is lost, the chasm is bridged,
you become one piece again—
but you regress to the animal world.
Love can also lead you to the Divine,
but then love has to be very, very meditative.
Then love has to be 'love plus meditation'.
That is what Tantra is—'Love plus meditation'.
You move into love, you allow your whole being total freedom,
but still, deep at the centre, you remain a witness.

If the witness is lost, you are going downhill;
if the witness remains there, then love, the same ladder,
can lead you to the very ultimate heaven.

Alcohol...all societies have been against it,
but still, they have to allow it,
because they know
that without alcohol there would be much chaos.
Alcohol has to be allowed in mild doses, legal doses;
legally it has to be allowed.
Why? Because it soothes people; it is a tranquilliser.
And people are in such an inner anguish,
they need something to soothe them.
Otherwise they would simply go berserk.
They would simply go mad.
So no society can afford freedom about alcohol,
but no society can prohibit it completely.
That is not possible. Either way it will be difficult to manage.
Alcohol is a need.
It is a need because the tension is so great inside
that you would go mad because of it.

And then many types of drugs have cropped up—
and it is not for the first time, it has been always so.
From the soma of Rig Veda to LSD 25, it has always been so.
Again and again drugs pop up.
Again they have to be pushed down, crushed;
and society tries to forget them.
But again they come back. There seems to be a deep need.
The need is:
a bridge is needed between the conscious and unconscious.
Unless a man becomes sincerely meditative,
drugs will be needed.
Unless you go upwards, you will have to fall downwards.

You cannot remain static.
This is one of the deeper laws of existence:
nobody can remain static.
Either he has to go up, or he has to fall down;
because life knows no rest, it knows only movement.
Either you go forward, or you will be thrown backward,
but you cannot say that you will stick to your state—
you will not go down and you will not go up.

No, that is not possible.
If you are not going up, you are already falling down—
you may or you may not know it.
Only a meditative society can be free of alcohol
and drugs, and other chemical ways to bridge the gap.

You can bridge the gap through being more alert,
that's why there is so much emphasis
on being alert, aware, witnessing, watchful.
Why? Because the more you become alert,
the more of the unconscious becomes conscious.
That is the only way.
If you remain more alert, if you walk with awareness,
if you talk, listen, with awareness,
if you eat, take your bath, with awareness,
not like a robot, not walking in sleep and doing things,
or doing things and thinking about other things
—that too is a sort of sleep—
no, if consciously, mindfully, you do your thing,
chunks of the unconscious
are being transformed into consciousness,
and by and by, more and more of your iceberg
comes out of the water of darkness, out of the ocean.

When the whole of you is out of darkness,
this is samadhi, this is enlightenment,
this is the state of a Buddha, or an *arhat:*
one who has no longer any unconsciousness in him,
one who has no longer any dark corners within his being.
The whole house is lighted.
Now, you have attained to a unity, you are crystallised.
Again, like the animal, you have unity—on a higher plane.
So a Buddha is pure like an animal, simple like an animal,
innocent like an animal—but not like an animal at all.
The animal has its innocence because of ignorance,
and Buddha has his innocence
because of his enlightened awareness.
The cause has changed.

This is the first thing, before we enter this story.

The second thing:

Awakening

a man comes to a point where he starts feeling
that suicide is the only way to get out of this whole mess.
This point comes in everybody's life—
when you are totally fed up with the struggle,
when you are totally bored with the whole effort of being.

Remember, just like suicide, boredom is also very special,
it is also human. No animal is ever bored.
Look at a buffalo, chewing grass, the same grass every day,
sitting and chewing and chewing, never bored.
You may get bored looking at her: she is not bored.
No animal is ever bored, you cannot bore an animal.
Too thick, too dense a mind—how can you bore?
For boredom a very, very high sensitivity is needed,
the higher your sensitivity, the higher will be your boredom,
the more will be your boredom.
Children are not bored;
they still belong more to the animal world than to the human,
they are human animals.
They still enjoy simple things, they are not bored.
Every day they can go hunting for butterflies
and they will never be bored—
and they are ready to go every day.
Have you ever talked to children, told them a story,
the same story? They will say: Tell it again.
And you tell it again and they will say: Tell it again.

You cannot bore children. You cannot bore animals.
Boredom is human, a very great quality, in fact,
because it exists only on a higher plane of consciousness.
When one is very sensitive one feels boredom—
life seems meaningless, there seems to be no purpose in it;
one feels as if it is just an accident,
whether you are here or not makes no difference.
The moment comes when one is so utterly bored
that one starts thinking of committing suicide.

What is suicide?
It is simply dropping out.
It is just saying that enough is enough.
I don't want to play the game again.
I want to drop out of the whole game.
Unless this point is reached, religion is not possible,

because only from this point can you either commit suicide,
or transform yourself. Here is the crossroad.

So this has been my observation:
people who become prematurely religious simply waste their time.
To become prematurely religious means to become religious
without being really fed up with life, not yet really bored.
The game still has some attraction.
It may be sex, it may be money, it may be politics, power.
But something in life still has an attraction.
Then prematurely you have become religious,
and this will not help: you will simply waste your time.
One has to be utterly bored; life has no more attraction;
all the dreams are shattered; all the rainbows have disappeared;
there are no more flowers, only thorns;
you are saturated with it.
Then there is no effort on your part
to leave it or renounce it—remember.
If there is any effort to renounce it,
it means there was a little attraction left.
Otherwise, what is the effort?
When you are fed up with a thing, do you renounce it?
No, there is no need to renounce. It is already renounced.

If you escape to the forest, from whom are you escaping?
From some attractions lingering in the world...
otherwise why? Where are you escaping to, and why?
Even in escape you are showing
that you are attached to something.
Remember this—this is the rule:
from wherever you escape, there is your attraction.
If you escape from woman, woman is your attraction.
If you escape from politics, politics is your attraction.
And the faster you run, the greater is the attraction.

This is premature, you will be called back.
You may go to the Himalayas, but you will think
that you have been chosen a president of a country.
You will dream.
Sitting in the Himalayas in this lonely cave, you will find
many *apsaras*, beautiful women, coming from heaven.
They are your mind's children.
Nobody is sending beautiful women to you:

Awakening

it is from woman that you have escaped.

Premature. There is no renunciation in a premature mind.
Maturity is needed, and maturity means you have lived life,
known it to the very depth, and found it lacking.
There is nothing in it, the journey is complete;
you can live in the market, or you can go to the monastery.
It doesn't matter, it is all the same.
Life is no longer an attraction:
wherever you are it makes no difference.
This point is the point of suicide.
And this point is the point of *sannyas*.
Suicide or *sannyas:* this is the alternative.
And, unless your *sannyas* is an alternative to suicide,
it is not very significant.

This is the point where you can feel the difference
between a religious mind and a secular mind.
A secular mind has no alternative.
When he is bored with life, suicide is the only way,
there is no alternative to it.

An atheist—what will he do when he is fed up with life?
He can commit suicide.
That's why in the West more suicide is committed.
That's why more men commit suicide than women.
The number is almost double because men
are more atheistic than women, less religious than women.
In the East less and less suicide is committed,
in the West more and more.
You go westwards, and you move into the hemisphere of suicide.

Great thinkers, philosophers, logicians,
commit suicide more than ordinary people,
because thinking implies doubt,
and a man who doubts, in fact becomes a believer in atheism.
You cannot remain in doubt because doubt is empty.
You have to cling to some belief—either in God, or no God;
either in the possibility of a future life,
or no possibility of a future life;
either in a meaning,
a transcendental meaning to higher planes,
or no higher planes;
but you have to decide. You cannot remain in doubt.

I have never seen anybody who lives in doubt.
He may call himself a sceptic: no, scepticism is his belief.
He may call himself an atheist—I don't believe in God—
but he believes in his non-belief.
And he believes as arrogantly as any theist;
and he is as ready to defend his belief
as any theist is ready to argue, to prove.
Nobody can live in doubt.

So there are two types of minds: secular and religious.
It will be good to understand the difference.
A secular mind believes in whatsoever is apparent,
whatsoever he can see, touch.
A religious mind believes not only in the apparent,
but in the transcendental.
The religious mind
is one which says that eyes cannot exhaust reality.
Reality is more than eyes can see.
Hands cannot clasp all that is: reality is more.
Ears cannot hear all that is: reality is more.
A religious mind says
that whatsoever you know is only a part—
there is a beyond, this life is not all.
There is more to life, there are more openings.
A secular mind is a closed mind;
a religious mind is an open mind—always ready to move,
always ready to probe, always ready to enquire,
always ready to travel to the unknown.
If you have a secular mind,
when you get fed up with life,
and you have lived all that life can give,
and you have found it useless, futile,
at the most a toy to be engaged with, occupied with
—and how long can you be occupied with a toy?—
then a moment comes, a moment of maturity,
when the toy has to be thrown away.
Then there is nothing.
This life was all, now it has flopped.
You can commit suicide. There is nothing else for you.

Only at the moment of suicide
does one come to know the beautiful world of religion.

And what the meaning of religion is, is only realised then.
Because this life is finished, but there is more life;
this world is finished, but the universe is vast;
this dimension has finished,
but there are millions of dimensions—
layers and layers and layers of being and existence.
There is no end to it.
This open mind is the religious mind,
and this vastness of possibilities is what is meant by God.
God is the infinite possibility for you to grow.
When one direction is finished, another direction opens.
In fact, whenever a door is closed, another opens immediately.

At this moment of suicide one stands at a crossroad:
either destroy yourself, or create yourself in a new way.
The old is no longer of any meaning.
Either destroy yourself completely—that is suicide—
or create yourself in a totally new way
so that you enter a new world, and a new life, and a new love.

A secular mind is simply destructive,
a religious mind is creative.
The religious mind says that when a world has finished
it shows simply that the way you lived,
the very base of your life, is finished—nothing else.
You can live in another way;
another style of being is possible. Create anew.
Up to now you have lived as a body, now you can live as a soul.
Up to now you have lived in a material way,
now you can live in a spiritual way.
Up to now you have lived
with greed and anger and sex, jealousy and possessiveness,
now live in a different way, non-possessive, in compassion.
Up to now you lived with greed as your base,
now live as a sharing, your whole being sharing with others.
Up to now you lived with thinking and thoughts and it failed,
now live as meditation, as ecstasy.
Up to now you were moving outwards and outwards and outwards
Now turn back.

This is the meaning of conversion:
turn back, move towards the source.
The outer has finished, the inner is there: now move inwards.

A new being arises.

Hindus have called this point the point of being reborn.
One birth is given by the parents—
that's the birth in the physical world.
Another birth is given by yourself—
that's the birth, the real birth, of your being.
Hindus call this rebirth,
and for the man who has attained to it
they have a particular name—
they call him *dwij*—twice born.
Out of his own womb he now gives a new birth to himself.
A new dimension opens: the dimension of meaning,
of significance, of eternal significance.
But it happens only
when you have come to such a bored state of being
that you would like to commit suicide.

Now, we will enter this beautiful Zen story.

*During three years of severe training
under the great master Gizan,
Koshu was unable to gain satori.*

Satori is samadhi, the first samadhi,
the very entrance into samadhi,
another world, totally unknown to you,
totally unimagined by you, not even dreamed of by you.
That world exists just by the side of this world.
In fact you have not to move even a single step:
just by the side of this world, just in it, it exists.
Only your viewpoint has to change.
Suddenly, when you have a new viewpoint
to look at the same world, another is revealed.
The world is your viewpoint, nothing else.
This world is ugly because your viewpoint is wrong.
If this world is just an anguish, a hell,
it is because your viewpoint is wrong.
It is not in fact the world which is a hell:
it is you who create hell around it; it is your projection.

The world is neutral, it is like a film screen—

clean, white, plain, pure.
And then it depends what you project on it.
You can project hell, you can project heaven—
or you may drop all projections. That is what *moksha* is.
Not projecting anything is the ultimate liberation.

*During three years of severe training
under the great master Gizan,
Koshu was unable to gain satori.*

Something has to be understood here.
If you don't make any effort, you will never attain,
but you can make too much effort also, and miss.
Sometimes you can overdo;
and this is a very, very delicate matter—
how to balance just in the middle.
It is easy not to do anything,
it is also easy to overdo a thing.
The difficult thing is just to be in the middle,
in the right proportion.

For the ego, extremes are easy.
Not to do anything is very easy,
then to do it too much is also easy.
People whose bodies have become too filled with fat
come to me and ask me what to do.
Should they go on a fast?
And I know that
either they can eat too much, obsessively,
or they can go on a fast. Both are easy.
But if you tell them to just cut their intake to half,
it is difficult. They can starve themselves,
that is not very difficult. Easy.
They can stuff themselves too much, that too is easy,
because in both cases they are doing harm to the body.
The quality of their murderous attitude towards the body
remains the same.
They can overstuff it: this is a sort of murder, violence.
Then they can do another type of violence:
they can go on a fast.
Both are extremes and both are wrong.
The extreme is always wrong.
To remain in the middle is always right.

This Koshu must have overdone things.
And it happens always that when you come to a master
you become infatuated.
When you are near a master you are so attracted by his being
that you would like to take a jump,
you would like to become like him,
you would like to do anything,
your activity becomes feverish—
you are in too much of a hurry.

Koshu must have done too much,
otherwise with a master like Gizan,
you can simply sit by his side and satori can happen.
Why three years of effort and he was still missing?
He had overdone it.

When you overdo a certain thing, anxiety is created;
when you overdo a certain thing, inner turmoil is created.
You are unbalanced, you cannot be at peace,
and satori happens only when you are at home.
In fact, satori happens only when you are really relaxed.

Do only that much which helps relaxation, don't overdo it.
And one has to feel his own way, because no fixed formula
can be given, because it differs and depends.
Each person has to find his own balance,
and, by and by, one becomes aware of what balance is.
Balance is a state of mind where you are silent,
no exertion, this way or that.

When you are lethargic and don't do much,
then your energy becomes a turmoil,
because too much energy inside will create restlessness.
Children are restless.
There is too much energy coming into their being
and they don't know what to do, where to throw it.
If you are lethargic,
you will have too much energy creating turmoil;
your own energy will become your enemy.
Or, if you become too active, do too much,
if you do a certain thing so much
that it drains your energy off, and you feel drained, tired,
then again you will be restless,
because you need a certain level of energy inside.

Either too much energy will create restlessness,
or, too drained of energy, you will feel restless.

With a master it almost always happens.
He has a magnetic centre in him, you become infatuated.
It is like a love affair—
you fall in love and then a fever arises.
Love is a sort of fever. The temperature goes high.

This must have happened to Koshu,
because after three years nothing happened.

*At the beginning of a special seven-day session of discipline,
he thought his chance had finally come.*

Every year, or every six months, or every three months,
they have a special seven-day discipline in Zen monasteries
called za-zen.
In these seven days one has to do nothing but meditate.
The whole energy has to be brought to it,
for seven days continuously,
only stopping for food—that too, very little—
and for two to three hours sleep in the night, that's all.
For the remaining twenty hours one has to meditate and meditate.
One has to sit for even six hours continuously
in a meditative posture, and meditate.
And when one feels completely tired, or sleepy,
and one cannot sit any more,
then one has to walk and meditate.
And in the whole seven-day session
the master is around you with his staff,
because when you meditate for three to four hours,
even half an hour is enough for one to start feeling sleepy.
So he hits you on the head with the staff.
Whosoever is feeling sleepy will be hit immediately
and brought back. Seven days of very strenuous effort....
That helps lethargic people.

But this Koshu must have been totally the opposite.
A session wouldn't help him, a special effort wouldn't help him:
he had been doing that already for three years.
In fact, he needed a different type of special meditation—
seven days of relaxation.

This has not existed in the Zen discipline.
It should, it has to, because there are two types of people:
the lethargic and the overactive.
For lethargic people it is good that for a few days
they should try their utmost; for lethargic people it is good.
But they are ninety-nine per cent,
that is why for the one per cent nobody has bothered.
For the one per cent, who have already been doing too much,
this session will not be of any help.

But...
*At the beginning of a special seven-day session of discipline,
he thought his chance had finally come.*
Now he would be doing all that he could do,
for almost twenty-four hours he would be meditating.
Now the satori could not escape his grasp.

*He climbed the tower of the temple gate,
and going up to the* arhat *images he made this vow:
Either I realise my dreams up here,
or they will find my dead body at the foot of this tower.*
Now he wanted to bring his total energy to it,
and he was sincere, he was serious.
He really wanted to have satori.
Even if his life had to be paid for it he was ready.
Either I realise my dreams up here,
he said in the tower, before the Buddha image,
or they will find my dead body at the foot of this tower.
He would commit suicide.

This is a point, a very rare point in life—
when you are ready to give so much, when you are really sincere.
Then suicide, or samadhi—this is the only alternative.

He went without food or sleep,
for seven days he didn't take any food, he didn't sleep,
giving himself up to constant za-zen...
za-zen is just sitting silently in a Buddha posture,
not doing anything, simply being aware;
no food, no sleep, just sitting for twenty-four hours.
He's doing his best, the last that he can do, the utmost.
...often crying out things like:

*What was my karma, that, in spite of all these efforts,
I can't grasp the way?*
The moment comes to every seeker, when he feels
that he is doing all that he can do, nothing more is possible.
*What was my karma that in spite of all these efforts
I can't grasp the way?*
But, in fact, he couldn't grasp the way
because of these efforts—
not in spite of them, *because* of them.

First, lethargy is the problem,
how to bring you out of your lethargy.
And then secondly, the problem is how to help you
to remain in the middle.
Not to move to the opposite end, the hyperactivity,
but to remain balanced.
Koshu had overdone it.
But that helped in a different way—through it
satori was never reached, through it he couldn't realise.
At last he admitted failure, and determined to end it all...
Now nothing was there, all that he could do he had done;
more he could not do, more was not there to be done.
So now there was no hope; for what to wait now?

At last he admitted failure...
This failure is not ordinary failure, it is not a failure
amid many failures, it is *the* failure.
When you fail in one thing it doesn't make any difference,
because there are many others you will succeed in.
When you fail in one effort,
you know that you can make another effort.
But this is *the* failure, because he had done
whatsoever he could do, more could not be done.
And there was nothing else: with life he was already finished,
now he had no more dates with life,
that game was completely over.
He had done everything that he could think of and do.
He accepted the failure—satori had not happened.

...and, determined to end it all...
so now suicide was the only possibility.
Samadhi was not there for him.
He could only commit suicide.

*...he went to the railing and slowly lifted his leg over it.
At that very instant he had an awakening.
The satori happened, the vast sky of samadhi opened immediately*

This has to be understood, because it may be the same for you.
This is not only one case, in many cases it has been so.
When you are a failure, a total failure,
many things happen within you—the ego evaporates.
Even in za-zen, sitting silently for seven days,
without food, without sleep, the ego was there.
In fact, who is asking for samadhi?
Who is there who asks that samadhi should happen?
This is the last effort of the ego;
the ego wants to grasp it, and that is the barrier.
When he accepted failure, the ego dissolved,
because the ego exists only with success.
Success is the food, the very stuff that the ego lives on.
If you are really a failure, a complete failure,
how can the ego remain there?
The ego cannot exist in ultimate failure.
The ego disappeared; and with the ego,
lethargy and hyperactivity, too much activity,
both disappeared. Without ego you are in the balance.
Suddenly, everything fits and you are in the balance.
Without ego there is no extreme, it cannot exist;
extreme exists as an ego effort.
Suddenly ego is not there and you are in the middle.
And now, the very effort of suicide is very, very balanced.

*At last he admitted failure, and, determined to end it all,
he went to the railing and slowly lifted his leg over it.*
Why slowly? Now, suicide was not really something
he was going to do:
suicide was something that was happening to him.
Finished with the world, there was no hurry also,
because he was not going to go anywhere,
he was simply dropping out of existence. There was no hurry.

Silently, slowly, he came to the railing.
This is really a beautiful moment, very deep.
Already this suicide is different.
You can commit suicide in very great hyper-tension—
that's how people commit suicide, in hyper-tension.

Awakening

If they are delayed, even for a single moment,
they will not commit suicide.
It has to be committed when you are completely mad;
it has to be done when really you are so tense
that you don't know what you are doing.
So, if you can delay suicide even for a single moment,
it will never happen.

I had a friend.
He was in love with a woman and the woman rejected him.
So, of course, being a poet, he thought of committing suicide.
His family was very disturbed.
They all tried to convince him; but the more they tried,
the more he became convinced
that he was going to commit suicide. This happens.
Not knowing what to do, they locked his door.
He started beating his head against the door.
They became very much afraid. What to do?

Suddenly they remembered me and called me. I went there.
He was beating his head against the door;
he was really in a fury and completely determined.
I went near the door and I said to him:
Why are you making so much show out of it?
If you want to commit suicide, do it. But why so much noise?
And why are you beating your head?
Just by beating your head on the door you will not die.
So, listen to me, come with me. We can go to the river,
there is a beautiful point where I have always meditated.
If ever I am to commit suicide, this is the place.
You come with me, this is a good chance.

Because I was not saying anything against suicide,
he calmed down. He was not hitting his head.
He was really puzzled, because you never expect
that your friend will help you to commit suicide.
So I told him: You open the door and don't make a fool
of yourself, and don't help crowds to gather here.
Why so much showmanship about it? You simply come with me
and drop yourself in the river. There is a waterfall
in the river and you will simply disappear.

So he opened the door and he looked at me,
he was very puzzled. I took his hand, brought him home.

He said: When are we going?
But he was a little afraid,
now that I was ready I was dangerous. So I said:
This is a full moon night and there is no hurry.
When one wants to die, one should choose an auspicious moment.
So we will go in the middle of the night,
then the full moon will be just there
and I can say good-bye and you can jump.
He became more and more afraid.
I was simply delaying the time.

We went to bed at ten o'clock. I fixed the alarm for twelve,
and I told him that sometimes I didn't hear the alarm,
so if he heard it first he should wake me.
Immediately the alarm started he put it off.
I waited for a few minutes then I said:
Why are you waiting? Wake me.
He became suddenly angry and said:
Are you my friend, or my enemy? It seems you want to kill me.
I said: I'm not making any judgement on my own.
If you want to die, I am a friend,
I have to co-operate and help.
If you don't want to die, that's your decision,
so you tell me. I am neutral.
The car is ready, I will drive you to the spot;
the night is beautiful and the moon has come up.
Now it is up to you.
He said: Take me to my home. I am not going to die.
And who are you to force me to die?

I was not forcing anybody—
just a delayed moment and one comes to one's senses.
But this is not that type of suicide.

I must tell you, by the way, that there is only one religion
in the world which allows suicide—Jainism.
It is rare; only Mahavir allows suicide.
He says that if you can die very silently,
without any emotionality about it, it is beautiful,
nothing is wrong with it.
But it has to be done over a very long time,
otherwise you never know.
So you have to stop taking food, that's all.

It takes almost three months for a person to die without food.
For three months the body goes on and on, using its reservoirs,
energy, and food and everything.
One goes on becoming more and more skinny,
the flesh disappears, then only the skeleton remains.
Nearly three months it takes.

So Mahavir says that if you want to die,
and if this suicide is going to be a religious dropping out,
then don't do it in a hurry.
Do it simply, because you have three months to think,
and you can go back, nobody is forcing you.
And there have been many people who have done it that way
in the past: many people have dropped out of existence
after not taking food for three months—
simply meditating, lying down.
Then that suicide is more beautiful than your ordinary life
because they are not really killing themselves,
they are moving to another realm.

This Koshu moved slowly, there was no hurry.
In fact, when life doesn't mean anything to you,
death also doesn't mean anything to you.
When life is useless, death is also useless,
because death is nothing but the culmination of life.
Death means so much to you because life means so much to you.
It is always in the same proportion.
If life is very, very meaningful to you,
you will be afraid of death.
When life is meaningless, of course death is also meaningless.
There is no hurry.

He came to the railing,
he went to the railing and slowly lifted his leg over it.
At that moment....
Just visualise the picture—a Buddhist monk
standing on a tower slowly lifting his feet,
and suddenly there is all that he always wanted to be.
The satori has happened, the lightning.

What happened in that moment?
Slowly lifting the leg up to commit suicide,
life was completely finished;

there was no greed in the mind, not even for satori.
There was no ego in the mind,
not even for religious achievement.
The future had completely dropped,
because it exists only with desires.
Desire is future, longing is future.
Only one longing had remained there inside him—for satori.
That longing was creating future and time,
that longing was the last barrier.
The last barrier had dropped.
Now there was no future, no desire. Only this moment existed.

At the moment when Koshu lifted his leg slowly,
all time stopped—no past, no future:
no past because life had been realised as useless;
no future because there was no longing, even for satori.

That leg lifted up, time stopped.
That leg lifted up, mind stopped—
because there was nothing to achieve, nothing to think.
At that moment he crossed out of time.
At that moment he transcended time.
At that moment his being became vertical, no longer horizontal.
No more past, no more future—all the waste disappeared.
At that moment of lifting, not only did he lift his leg,
his whole being was lifted up.
The vertical dimension started.
And suddenly, there was satori.

Suddenly, *at that very instant, he had an awakening.*

It always happens so:
it happened in the same way to Buddha himself.
He left the world, the palace,
the beautiful wife, the newly born child, the whole empire.
The world was no longer meaningful.
Then for six years he tried and tried and tried his utmost.
He went to every teacher,
to every master that he came to know about.
And he said: I am ready to do whatsoever,
but I want to know what life is, who I am.
And the masters, many masters in those six years,

Awakening

told him to do many things, and he did them.
And he did them so perfectly that no master could tell him
that it was not happening because he was not doing well.
That was impossible—
even the master was not as perfect as the disciple.
So the masters accepted their failure,
and they said that up to this moment, to this extent,
they could help; beyond this they themselves didn't know.
So he should seek another master.
Then all the masters were finished.

Then he started doing things on his own;
and he did everything that was prevalent in India for centuries.
He tried all methods of hatha yoga, raja yoga.
He did everything that was available. He overdid it.
He was too anxious to achieve. He was too serious about it.
His sincerity became a hyper-tension inside,
and he couldn't attain.

Then one day, crossing the Niranjana River near Bodh Gaya,
he was so weak because of fasting that he couldn't cross it.
It was a very small stream but he couldn't swim it,
and he had to hang onto a root of a tree to save his life.
He was so weak.
In that moment he thought:
What have I done? I have destroyed my body
and I have not attained to any soul;
this whole effort has been foolish.

At that moment he dropped all efforts.
The world was already useless,
now the religious world of efforts was also useless.
On that day he relaxed under a tree,
which became the Bodhi Tree
under which he attained his enlightenment.
He relaxed. That relaxation was total.
For the first time, there was nothing to achieve:
the achieving mind dropped.
He had done everything and nothing more could be done.
So what to do? He simply slept.

That night there was no dream,
because when there is no desire there is no dream.
Dreams are the shadows of desires. Dreams are desires

which go on haunting you even in your sleep.
The whole night passed as if it was a single moment.

And in the morning, the early morning,
when the last star was disappearing,
he opened his eyes and looked at the star.
He was in the same situation as Koshu was
when Koshu lifted his leg and was going to drop himself
from the tower.
The disappearing last star—
and he opened his eyes with no mind inside, with no desire
Time stopped—and suddenly, it was there.
His longing was the barrier.

So, one has to long first, and one has to strive,
and one has to make all the efforts,
and one has to roam, and seek and enquire,
and one has to do whatsoever one can do,
and then, one has to drop all.

You cannot drop it right now,
because you have nothing to drop.
First you have to do, then you can drop.
You can go to a tower, and you can raise your leg
very, very slowly, but nothing will happen.
Because it is not a question of the outer posture—
for the inner you have not yet done all that has to be done.
You can go to a Bodhi tree and lie down, completely relaxed,
and in the morning, exactly when the last star is disappearing,
you can open your eyes. Nothing will happen.

One has to pass through arduous effort
to come to a total relaxation.
Then suddenly it happens.
In fact it has been always there around you;
only you were not there. You were not present.
You were moving in the mind, in the desires, in the future,
in the past, in the memories, in the thoughts.
You were too attached to clouds,
that's why you couldn't see the sky.
It was always there.
In fact the clouds were roaming in the sky.
Samadhi is all around you; samadhi is the ocean.

Awakening

And you are the fish—but you are not present.

Overjoyed, he rushed down the stairs and through the rain to Gizan's room.

Before he had a chance to speak, the master cried: Bravo!—you have finally had your day.

The very quality of the person
who has attained to satori changes.
He need not say—at least to the master—
he need not say: I have achieved.
Because the very vibration,
the very being of one who has achieved, is totally different.
Even before he could say anything, the master said:
Bravo! So you have achieved, so it has happened.
There was no need to talk about it.
Once it happens, those who know will see it.
Even those who don't know will start to feel it.

You cannot come to a man of realisation
without feeling something of the unknown,
without listening to his footsteps
in the world of the unknown, in the world of the mysterious.
Mystery surrounds him.
In his very shadow a very sacred quality exists.
In his very movement there is a holiness, because he is whole.
Satori makes you whole; samadhi makes you whole.
Now there is no longer a division
between conscious and unconscious.
Suddenly it is bridged. The whole has become conscious.

The quality is just like this:
you see a house in the night, with no light within.
Then somebody lights a lamp inside.
The whole quality of the house changes;
even passers-by on the road will suddenly see
that the light is burning in the house.
The quality has changed.
From the windows, from the doors, from the cracks,
the light is shining to the outside.
The house is no longer dark.

Not a Dead One
27th February 1975

*An ex-emperor asked the master Gudo:
What happens to a man of enlightenment
after death?*

*Gudo replied:
How should I know?*

*The ex-emperor said:
Why?—because you are a master.*

*Gudo said:
Yes, sir, but not a dead one!*

Man is ignorant of the real.
And it is difficult to know the real
because, to know the real, first you have to be the real.
Only the same can know the same.

Man is false. As man exists, he is a deep hypocrite.
He is not real himself. His original face is completely lost.
He has many faces, he uses many faces,
but he himself is not aware of the original face: his own.

Man is an imitator.
He goes on imitating others,
and, by and by, he completely forgets
that he has his own unique being.

The real can be known only when you are real.
It is a tremendous effort; arduous is the path.
So man tries a trick.
He starts thinking about the real—
philosophising, theorising,
creating mental systems about the real.
That is all that philosophy is:
a trick of the mind to deceive oneself about one's ignorance,
about one's not knowing the real.
That's why philosophies abound
and the whole world lives in concepts and theories.
Hindus, Mohammedans, Christians, Jains, Buddhists—
there are millions of concepts.

And they are cheap, you need not change yourself;
you need only an ordinary intelligent mind, a mediocre mind.
No higher IQ is needed, so there is not any difficulty.
You can adopt concepts
and you can hide your ignorance from yourself.
Philosophy is just a hiding method:
one starts feeling that one knows, without knowing at all;
one starts feeling that one has arrived,
without even having taken the first step.

Philosophy is the greatest disease,
and once you are caught in it
it is very difficult to come out of it
because it is so deeply fulfilling to the ego.
One feels hurt when one comes to know one's ignorance.
And ignorance is total and absolute;
you don't know anything at all.
You are simply in dark ignorance, and this hurts.
One would like to know something, at least something,
and philosophy gives you a consolation: there are theories,
and if you have an ordinary intelligence, that will do—
you can learn the theories,
you can have your own system, a philosophy,
and then you are at ease.
Then not only do you know, but you can teach others,
you can advise others,
you can go on showing your knowledge to others—
and everything is settled, ignorance is forgotten.

Philosophy means a logical construction about reality:
it is about and about and about,
it is never the real.
Round and round it goes, just beating around the bush,
but it never hits the centre of the real.
It cannot do that, that is not possible for philosophy.
Why is it not possible?
Because philosophy is based on logic,
and reality is beyond logic.

You have to understand it a little more.

Logic is a search for consistency,
and reality is not consistent.
Or, it is so deeply consistent
that even the opposite is not inconsistent with it.
Reality is paradoxical:
all the opposites meet and mingle and merge into it.
It is so vast.
Logic is narrow; logic is like a road, narrow, goal-oriented.
Reality is like a vast space, no goal, not going anywhere;
it is already there, moving in all dimensions together.
Logic is one dimensional, reality is multi-dimensional.
Logic says A is A and can never be B
—this is the consistency of logic—
and in reality, A is A, but always moves and becomes B also.

Logic says life is life and can never be death.
How can life be death?
But in reality, life is moving every moment into death.
Life is death.

Logic says love is love and can never be hate;
but love is moving every moment into hate,
and hate is moving every moment into love.
You love the same person and you hate the same person—
the deeper the love, the deeper the hate.
Hate and love are two aspects of the same coin.
Can you hate a person without loving him?
How can you hate a person without loving him?
First you have to love, only then can you hate.
Hate needs love as a first step.
How can you become inimical to a person
with whom you have never been friendly?

Friends and foes are separate only in logic;
in reality they are together.
If you search your hate deeply, you will find love hidden.

The moment you are born, death is also born with you.
Birth is the beginning of death,
and death is the culmination of birth.
Says Heraclitus:
God is life and death,
summer and winter,
hunger and satiety,
good and bad.

Always both.
And God is reality.

If you look at reality, you will see all opposites meeting.
Reality is contradictory; logic is non-contradictory.
Logic is clean, plain, simple; reality is very complex.
Reality is not like a logical syllogism
or a mathematical problem—it has many dimensions.
And it is interrelated, all contradictions are together:
the day turns into night, the night again turns into day.
The morning is nothing but the indication
that the evening is coming.
Youth becomes old age. Beauty turns and becomes ugly.
Everything changes, and becomes the opposite.

This has to be understood deeply,
because this is the basic difference
between philosophy and religion.
Philosophy is logical; religion is not.
Philosophy is logical; religion is real.
To understand philosophy is not difficult;
to understand religion is almost impossible.
Logic speaks a plain language; religion cannot speak,
because religion has to speak the language of the reality.

Logic is a fragment chosen from reality by the mind,
it is not total.
Religion accepts the whole and wants to know it as it is.
Logic is a mental construction.
Philosophy, logic, science, all are mental constructions:
they are all based on logic.

Not a Dead One

Religion is a de-structuring of the whole mind.
Philosophy is a structure of the mind about the reality,
a creation of a system. The mind remains there
and helps you to choose, to project, to find.
In religion you have to de-structure the mind.
The reality remains as it is,
you don't do anything to the reality—
you simply drop the mind, and then you look.
If the mind is there, it won't allow you to look at the whole.
The mind is obsessed with consistency,
it cannot allow the contradictory.

So, whenever you come near a person who is enlightened,
your mind will be in difficulty,
you will feel many contradictions in him.
Your mind will say:
This man says this, and then he contradicts.
And sometimes he says this, and then again something else—
he is inconsistent.
A religious man is,
by the very nature of the case, contradictory;
he has to be,
because he is not in search of consistency,
he is in search of the truth.
He is in search of the real,
and he is ready to drop everything for the real,
whatsoever the real is.
He has no preformulated structure for the real—
he has no idea how the real should be.
If it is inconsistent, it is inconsistent. Okay.
He has nothing to impose on it.
A religious mind simply allows the real to reveal itself.
He has no idea how it should be.

A religious man is passive;
a logical, philosophical, scientific man is aggressive.
He gets some idea and, through that idea,
he structures reality.
Around the idea he tries to discover the real.
The idea won't allow you to discover the real—
the very idea is the hindrance.

So one path is logic, another path is poetry.

Poetry is against logic.
Logic is rational, poetry is irrational.
Logic is logical, poetry is imagination.
And this distinction has to be remembered
because religion is neither—
neither logic, nor poetry.

Logic is of the mind and imagination is also of the mind.
A poet imagines reality.
Of course, his reality is more colourful
than a logician's reality,
because he imagines, and he is not afraid.
He is completely free in his imagination,
he has not to follow any idea.
He simply dreams about reality: but it is again 'about'.
He dreams about reality,
he makes a beautiful whole out of his dreaming.
He is colourful, because deep down is fantasy.
Logic is plain, colourless, almost grey;
there is no poetry in it
because there is no imagination in it.
Poetry is almost contradictory, because it is imagination.
It doesn't bother.
You never ask the poet to be consistent.
If a poet writes one poem today, another tomorrow,
and contradicts himself, nobody bothers.
People say this is poetry.

If a painter paints a certain thing today,
and just the opposite tomorrow,
you don't ask for any consistency, you don't say:
What are you doing? Yesterday you painted the moon yellow
and today you are painting the moon red.
What are you doing? You are contradicting.
No! Nobody asks—it is poetry,
painting is poetry, sculpture is poetry,
and you allow the poet all freedom.
But poetry is imagination.

Mind has two centres:
one is thinking, another is imagination.
But both centres are of the mind—
and religion is beyond, beyond both centres,
it is not of the mind at all.

Not a Dead One

It is neither science nor poetry—or it is both.
That's why religion is a deeper mysticism than any poetry.
It simply drops the mind, with all its centres,
and then looks.
It is just as if you put aside your glasses, and look.
The mind can be put aside because it is a mechanism;
you are not the mind.
The mind is just like a window.
You are standing there and looking through the window,
then the frame of the window becomes the frame of reality.
You look from the window,
the moon has arisen, and the sky is beautiful,
but your sky will be framed by the window.
And if the window has certain colours of glass,
then your sky will be coloured by the window.

Religion is simply coming out of the house completely;
looking at reality,
not through any window, not through any door,
not through any glasses, not through any concepts,
but simply looking at it as it is, putting aside the mind.
It is difficult because you are so identified with the mind
that you have completely forgotten that you can put it aside.
But this is the whole methodology of religion:
all of yoga, tantra, and all the techniques of meditation
are nothing but how to put the mind aside,
how to break the identity with the mind, and then look.
Then whatsoever is reality is revealed:
that which is, is revealed. Remember this.

Sometimes religion will speak the language of logic,
then it becomes theology.
Sometimes religion will speak the language of poetry,
then it becomes objective art, like the Taj Mahal.
If you go and watch the Taj Mahal for the first time,
you will understand what objective art is.
Looking at a piece of objective art, like the Taj Mahal,
if you simply sit and watch and look,
suddenly a silence surrounds you, a peace descends upon you.
The very structure of the Taj Mahal
is related to your innermost being;
just looking at the shape of it, something changes within you.

There are two types of art.
One art is subjective—for example, Picasso.
If you look at a Picasso painting
you can understand what type of mind Picasso must have had,
because he pictures, paints his own mind,
and he must have been living in nightmares,
because all his painting is nightmarish.
You cannot look at it for long without feeling ill and nauseous.
It is his inner madness that he has painted in colour,
and it is infectious.
This is subjective art:
whatsoever you do, you bring in your own mind.

Objective art is not bringing your own mind in,
but following some objective rules
to change the person who will look at it, meditate on it.

All of Eastern art has tried to be objective.
The artist is not involved in it,
the painter is forgotten, the sculptor is forgotten,
the architect is forgotten, they are not involved in it.
They are simply following certain objective rules
to create a piece of art,
and for centuries, whenever somebody looks at it,
something of meditation will happen in them.
On a full moon night, sitting near the Taj Mahal,
not talking, just meditating on it,
time disappears, a no-time moment happens.
And suddenly the Taj Mahal is not there outside,
something is changing within you.

Sometimes religion talks in terms of objective art,
to bring the reality into this world of the mind.
Sometimes it talks in terms of logic,
then it becomes theology, then it argues.
But these are both compromises with the world,
compromises with the ordinary, mediocre mind,
bringing religion to the ordinary mind.
When religion speaks in its purity it is paradoxical,
like the 'Tao-te-Ching' of Lao Tzu,
or the fragments of Heraclitus, or these Zen stories.
In its purity religion transcends logic, imagination, both.
It is the very beyond.

Not a Dead One

Now, a few things about the 'very beyond',
then we can enter into this story.

It is small, like a seed.
But if you allow it the soil of your heart,
it can grow into a vast tree.
It is small, if you look at the form;
but if you look at the formless hidden in it,
it has no limits, it is infinite.

Something to be aware about the very beyond—
first, the very beyond, the transcendental,
needs a transformation in you,
otherwise you will not be able to understand it.
It needs a clarity of perception in you.
It is not a question of intellect alone;
even a genius may not be able to understand it, and sometimes
even an ordinary villager may be able to understand it.
Sometimes even an Einstein may miss it,
because it is not a question of cleverness, intelligence—
it is a question of clarity, not cleverness.
Clarity is different.
Cleverness is a way of being cunning with reality;
it is cunningness.
Clarity is completely different;
it is not cunningness, it is innocence, child-like.
You don't have a mind, the window is completely open.
You don't have any ideas, because a mind filled with ideas
loses its clarity; it is just like a sky filled with clouds.
A mind filled with thoughts is not transparent,
it is a junkyard. And through that junkyard,
you cannot come to realise what reality is.
One has to clean oneself. A deep cleansing is needed.
One has to pass through many meditations
so that, by and by, your mind becomes clear,
like a clear sky with no clouds.
So it is not a question of intellectual understanding,
it is a question of a different type of being,
a being who is clear, like a clear sky.

The second thing to remember is
that a religious mind never goes beyond the moment,
because the moment you go beyond the moment
you have started working through the mind.

The future is not here, so how can you look at it?
You can only think about it.
You can only think about the future, you cannot see it.
Only the present moment can be seen, it is already here.
So the religious mind lives in the moment;
you cannot force the religious mind to go beyond the moment,
because the moment the religious mind thinks about the future,
it is no longer religious.
Immediately the quality of the mind has changed.
The religious mind exists here and now,
and that is the only way to exist.
If you think about the future, the moment that is not here,
you are already in the trap of the mind
and you have allowed thoughts to form.
In the present there is no thought.
Have you ever observed this?
Right now, how can thought exist?
No thought ever exists in the present,
it always exists in the future or in the past.
Either you think of the past—then there is imagination;
or you think of the future—then there is logic.
How can you think of the present?
You can only be.
And the moment is so subtle, so small, so atomic,
that there is no space for any thought to exist in it.
Thought needs space, needs room,
and in the present there is no room for thought.
Only being can be there.
So whenever you are in the present, thinking stops,
or, if you stop thinking you will be in the present.
A religious mind is not concerned about the future,
is not concerned about what happened in the past.
It lives in the moment and it moves from moment to moment.
When this moment disappears, another moment comes:
the religious man has moved into it. He is river-like.

The very, very deep thing to be remembered is that
a religious mind, a religious man, a religious being,
is always a process, he is always moving.

Of course, the movement is unmotivated.
It is moving not for any goal, it simply moves—
because movement is the nature of reality.

Not a Dead One

Movement is the nature of reality, it moves with reality,
just as somebody floats with the river.
He moves with the river of time.
Each moment he lives, and moves.
He is not doing anything, he simply lives the moment.
When the moment has gone, another comes: he lives that moment.
A religious man has a beginning but no end;
awakening has a beginning, but no end—
it goes on and on and on.

Just the opposite is the case with ignorance—
ignorance has no beginning, but an end.
Can you say when your ignorance started? It has no beginning.
When did Buddha's ignorance start?
It had no beginning, but it had an end.
It ended on a certain full moon night,
twenty-five centuries ago.
Ignorance has an end, but no beginning;
enlightenment has a beginning, but no end.
And that's how the circle becomes complete.
When an ignorant man becomes enlightened
the circle is complete.

Ignorance has no beginning, but has the end;
enlightenment has the beginning, but has no end.
Now the circle is complete.
Now here is the perfect being whose circle is complete.

But this perfection doesn't mean any 'staticness',
because enlightenment has no end;
it goes on and on and on, for eternities, for ever.

Now, try to understand this beautiful seed-like story.

An ex-emperor asked the master Gudo:
What happens to a man of enlightenment after death?

If he had asked philosophers
they would have supplied many answers.
The scriptures are full of answers.

What happens to an enlightened man after death?
Buddha was asked the same question again and again,

and he would simply laugh sometimes.
Once it happened that it was evening
and a small earthen lamp was burning near Buddha.
Somebody asked the question:
What happens to a man of enlightenment after death?
Buddha put the flame out, and asked:
What happens now to the flame which is no more?
Where has it gone? Where is it now?
Just a moment before it was here, now where has it gone?
The same thing happens to the man of enlightenment.

This is not an answer.
The man must have gone unsatisfied,
feeling that Buddha was avoiding the question.

Those who have known have always avoided,
but those who don't know, they have many answers.
Scholars, pundits, you ask them
and they will supply many answers.
You can choose any of your liking.

Gudo replied:
How should I know?
You are asking something of the future, and I am here and now.
For me there is no future.
Only this moment exists, there is no other moment.
You are talking about death, death of an enlightened person,
somewhere in the future, or somewhere in the past.
What happened to Buddha?

That's why Gudo said: *How should I know?*
He means:
I am here and now; no past is meaningful for me, no future.
He is saying:
Look at me right now. The enlightened being is before you.
He is saying:
Look at me. Why are you concerned?

It happened once that a man came to meet Gudo
—he was a very famous master—
and the man was very old, near about ninety.
He belonged to a particular Buddhist sect.
And he said: I have come from very far,
and my life is almost coming to an end,

Not a Dead One

and I have always been waiting for a chance to meet you
—because Gudo was known all over the country
as the master of the emperor—
before I die I have come to you
because I have to ask you one question.
For almost fifty years I have been studying the scriptures,
and I have come to know everything.
Only one thing disturbs me. In my scriptures it is written
that even trees and rocks will become enlightened.
That I could never understand. Trees and rocks?
Gudo said: Tell me one thing.
Have you ever thought about yourself?
Can you become enlightened, or not?
The man said: It is strange,
but I must confess that I never thought about it.

Trees and rocks and how they can become enlightened—
he had been thinking about this for fifty years!
And he had come from far away to ask this question of Gudo,
and he had never thought about himself.

People talk about death,
not knowing that right now they are alive.
Life is here, first know it. Live it totally!
Why do you talk about death?

People talk about what will happen after death.
It would be better to think about what is happening to you
right now, after birth. And when death comes, we will meet it.
First meet life that is here now; and if you can meet life,
you will become capable of meeting death also.
One who can live rightly will die rightly.
One who has lived a total, rich life
of moment to moment moving, living, awareness, consciousness,
will of course, when death comes, do the same with death.
He will live it,
because he knows the quality of how to live in the present.
When death becomes the present, he will live it.
But people are more concerned about death,
less concerned about life.
But if you cannot know life,
how do you suppose that you will be able to know death?
Death is not separate from life,

it is the very culmination of it.
If you miss life, you will not be able to see death.
Death will come, but you will be unconscious.

That is what is happening.
People die in a deep unconsciousness, a coma.
They live their whole life in unconsciousness,
and when you treated life with unconsciousness,
how do you suppose
that you will be able to be conscious before death?
Death will happen in a single moment,
and life is a seventy or eighty year process.
If you could not even become aware in eighty years,
if eighty years were not enough for you to become conscious,
how will you be able to in one second?
Only a person who has lived moment to moment
will be able to see death,
because when he has lived life moment to moment,
death cannot escape him.
He has the clarity, such intense clarity,
that even in a single moment, when death comes and moves,
he will be able to see it.
One who has been able to see life,
will automatically be able to see death—
and then one knows one is neither life nor death.
One is just the witness.

When a person asks
what happens to a man of enlightenment after death
he himself is not enlightened. He is asking
from his deep ignorance, so it is difficult to answer.
It is just like a blind man asking what happens
when the sun rises in the morning.
How to explain that to him?
How to make the communication? It is impossible.

It once happened that a man was blind,
not only blind, he was a great philosopher.
The whole village was disturbed by him,
because he proved logically that there is no light.
He said: I have hands. I can touch and feel.
So show me where light is.
If something exists, it can be touched;

Not a Dead One

if something exists, it can be tasted;
if something exists, and you hit something against it,
I can hear the sound.

And the villagers were very disturbed,
because they couldn't gather any proof.
He had four senses and he said:
I have four senses. You bring light before me
and I will see through my four senses
whether it is there or not.
And they said: Because you are blind, you cannot see.
He laughed and said: It seems that you are dreaming.
What are eyes? And how can you prove that you have eyes
and I don't have? You tell about your light, what it is.
Explain it to me.
They couldn't do that. It was impossible.
But they felt very depressed,
because this man was blind and they had eyes,
and they knew what light was. But how to explain to a blind man?

Then Buddha came to the town.
They all took this mad philosopher, the mad blind man,
to Buddha and they asked Buddha:
You try to explain to him, we have failed.
And this man is something: he has proved
that light is not there because it cannot be touched,
cannot be smelled, cannot be tasted, cannot be heard.
So how can it exist? Now you have come, you can explain to him.
Buddha said:
You are fools! Light cannot be explained to a blind man.
The very effort is absurd.
But I know a man who is a great physician.
You take this man to him, and he will treat his eyes.

The man was taken to the physician, his eyes were treated.
He was not really blind. Within six months he started seeing.
Then he came running to Buddha, who was now in another town.
He fell at his feet and he said:
Yes, now I know. Light is.
Now I know why those poor villagers could not prove it,
and now I also know that you did well to send me to a physician.
I needed treatment—not philosophy, not theories about light.

When an ignorant person asks,

'What happens to an enlightened person after death?' leave it.
Even, 'What happens to an enlightened man while he is alive?'
cannot be explained. *Cannot* be explained.
What has happened to me? How can I explain it? No possibility.
It is impossible—unless you start seeing, unless your eyes open.
Unless you are changed, nothing can be explained.
The communication is not possible,
because enlightenment is a totally different quality of being,
and you are completely blind to it.
You can believe that I am enlightened, but you cannot see it.
That belief will help,
because that belief will allow you to remain open.
That trust will help, because you can deny, you can say:
No, I cannot believe. How can I believe?
How can I trust when I don't know?
That will close you: then there is no possibility.
That's why religion insists on trust, *shraddha*.
The blind man can only believe and trust
when people say that light exists.
And if he trusts, then there is a possibility.
If he does not trust, then he will not even allow a treatment.
He will say: What are you doing? There is no light,
and there are no such things as eyes. I don't believe you,
so please don't waste your time, and don't waste my time.

It is impossible to communicate
from one plane to another plane; it won't function at all.
You have to rise up to another plane of being;
only then, suddenly, can you see.
And when you see and experience, then the trust is fulfilled.
But before you see, one has to have faith, to have trust,
just to allow the transformation.

Gudo replied:
How should I know?
Death has not come yet. When it comes, it comes.
Then I will know and I will inform you,
but right now I don't know.

An enlightened person will not give you theories.
He would like to give you insight, not theories.
Insight is a deep phenomenon within you;

theory is just borrowed.
He could have replied, because there are theories
about what happens to the enlightened man.
Some say he reaches to a plane called *moksha*,
where he lives for ever and ever.
Some are more colourful,
they say he goes to the kingdom of God
and lives with God for ever and ever,
just like Jesus sitting by the throne of God,
on the right hand, with angels dancing and singing
and celebrations going on and on.
There are millions of theories.
But they are all created by the theologians to console people.
You ask—so somebody has to give you the answer.

But not enlightened people: they have remained silent about it.
They are not concerned at all.
Jesus says: Consider the lilies of the field.
They exist only here and now.
They don't bother about the tomorrow;
the tomorrow will take care of itself.

Somebody brought the New Testament to a Zen master,
and he read a few sentences from it—
particularly this sentence:
Consider the lilies in the field. They toil not,
they don't think of the morrow,
and they are so beautiful in the here and now
that even Solomon, the great emperor, in his peak glory,
was not arrayed in such beauty.
When he read this the Zen master said:
Stop! Whosoever said this is a Buddha.
He didn't know about Jesus, he didn't know about Christianity.
Christianity had reached Japan just a few days before.
The master said: Stop! No need to say anything more.
Whosoever said this is a Buddha.

All enlightened persons have insisted
on remaining in the moment.
That's why Gudo said: How should I know?

The ex-emperor said:
Why?—because you are a master.

From a master we expect answers,
but in fact, a master never gives you an answer,
he simply destroys your question.
There is a vast difference between these things.
From a master we expect answers to our questions,
but if the questions are foolish, the answers cannot be better.
How can you answer a foolish question ir a wise way?
The very question is foolish.
Somebody comes and asks:
What is the taste of the colour green?
It is absurd, because there is no relationship.
But the question looks perfect, linguistically it is perfect.
You can ask: What is the taste of the colour green?
There is no error in the language, in the formulation.

The same is the case, for many reasons, when somebody asks:
What happens to an enlightened person when he is dead?
First, he is never dead. An enlightened person
is one who has come to know the eternal life.
He is never dead.
Second, an enlightened person is no longer a person.
His ego is dissolved, that's why he is enlightened.
So, in the first place, he is never dead;
in the second place, he is already dead, because he is no more.

Buddha moved about for forty years after his enlightenment,
but in those forty years,
while he was wandering from village to village,
talking to people continuously,
giving them whatsoever he has attained,
it is said that he never uttered a single word
and he never took a single step.
What does this mean?
It is rightly said that he never uttered a single word,
because he was no more.
How can you utter a word when you are not?
It was as if existence itself, not Buddha, uttered those words,
because now Buddha was no longer a person,
just the name remained, utilitarian, functional.
Otherwise there was no need for it.
He never took a single step, but he was wandering and wandering.
The whole province of Bihar is called 'Bihar'
because of his wanderings. Bihar means the wandering,

Not a Dead One

and because he was wandering there,
the whole province is known as Bihar.
But it is said that he never took a single step
—and it is right, absolutely right—
he never took a single step.

I tell you: I continuously talk to you
but I have not uttered a single word.
When the ego is not there, who can utter?
Then what is happening when I am talking to you?
It is just like a breeze passing through the trees;
it is just like a spring moving towards the river;
it is just like a flower opening.
But I am not there.
And the flower cannot claim that it opened itself.
The breeze cannot say: I pass through these trees,
because the breeze has no ego to say it.
The river cannot say: I am moving towards the ocean.
The river moves, but there is nobody who is moving.
I talk to you, but I have not uttered a single word.

But, how to communicate these things?
An enlightened person is already dead;
the past has disappeared, the centre is no longer there.
Now he is nowhere—he exists everywhere.
Now he is one with the whole,
the wave has lost itself into the ocean.
So, when you see Buddha standing there,
that body is just a contact point, that's all. Nothing else.
It is just like an electricity plug. If you plug in there
the energy moves: otherwise the energy is everywhere.
So, when Buddha is standing there,
he is just a contact point for the cosmos.
He is no longer there, he is just a passage,
just an anchor into this world. And when the anchor is lost,
that's when Buddha's body will drop.

You ask: What happens?
When a wave is no more, what happens? It becomes the ocean.
When a Buddha is no more,
the body disappears like the wave has disappeared.
Buddha is already dead, that's why he is a Buddha;
and secondly, he can never die,

because once the ego is lost, the eternal life is attained.
Now Buddha is not anywhere: he is everywhere.
When you don't have a centre,
the whole existence becomes your centre.

The question is foolish.
It looks logical, meaningful, but it is foolish.
That's why Gudo replied: *How should I know?*
Many things are implied.
Gudo is saying: I am not. Who should know?
When the wave disappears in the ocean, how should I know?

The ex-emperor said:
Why?—because you are a master.

We expect answers from a master,
but answers are given by teachers, not by masters.
Masters simply destroy your mind;
even if it appears that they are answering you,
they never answer. They are elusive.
You ask something, they talk about something else.
You ask about A, they talk about B.
But they are very persuasive, seductive. They talk about B
and they convince you that, yes, your question is answered.
But your questions are foolish, they cannot be answered,
they are irrelevant.
So a master never answers the questions.
He gives you the feeling that he is answering you,
but he is simply trying to pull the earth
from beneath your feet.
The whole effort is for your mind to fall, to collapse.
If you can be near a master for a little while,
you will collapse.
He is a chaos; you will be pulled down completely.
Neither questions nor answers will be there.
Only then, when silence exists in you,
has a master succeeded with you.

Answers will fill your mind again,
so how can a master give you answers? They will be theories,
they won't allow you to enter into reality.
A master really cuts away your questions
until, by and by, you stop asking,

and when the moment of no asking comes,
only then is the answer given.
But that answer is not verbal;
that answer is from his very being.
Then the master pours himself into you.
He is the vehicle, and the whole pours through him into you.

Why?—because you are a master.

We think that a master must be very knowledgeable,
that he must know everything.
In fact a master knows nothing:
he has attained to perfect ignorance,
because only ignorance can be innocent, knowledge never.
Knowledge is always cunning, it can never be innocent.
Perfect ignorance. He does not know anything.
Knowledge has dropped. He is, but he is not a knower,
and whatsoever he says is out of his innocence,
not out of his knowledge.
He can say millions of things, because innocence is so potent.
He can go on and on for years—for forty years Buddha talked.
Now scholars say that it seems impossible for one man
to talk for forty years—and about so many things.
It seems a difficult thing for them
because they don't know that innocence is inexhaustible.
Knowledge will be exhausted.
If I know something, it is limited,
then I cannot go on and on and on.
And I tell you
that if you are ready, I can go and on for eternity,
because it is not out of knowing, but out of perfect ignorance.

Perfect ignorance is not your ignorance:
your ignorance is not perfect.
You know—in fact you know too much.
You cannot find an ignorant person who doesn't know.
He may know less, more, but he knows;
he may know, wrongly or rightly, but he knows.
Even an idiot knows, and insists that he knows rightly.
Only an enlightened man denies that he knows.
Said Socrates: When I was young,
I knew many things, in fact I knew all.
Then I became a little more mature and I started feeling

that I didn't know much, in fact, very little.
And when I became very, very old
then I understood the whole thing.
Now I know only one thing: that I don't know.

While he was young he knew many things. . . .
Youth is arrogant.
Only immature persons are knowledgeable;
maturity is like ignorance, it doesn't know.
Or it knows only that it doesn't know.

Gudo replied:
How should I know?

The ex-emperor said:
Why?—because you are a master.

Answers are expected.
He must know. If he doesn't know, then who else will know?

And beautiful is Gudo—
Said he: *Yes, sir, but not a dead one!*
I am a master, but not a dead one.
Wait. When I am dead, then I will say what happens
when an enlightened person dies.
I am yet alive and you ask me about death.
It has not happened, so how should I know?
When it happens, I will report to you.

It never happens to an enlightened man.
Gudo is really clever. It never happens to an enlightened man.
Only ignorant people die. Only the egos die.
When there is no centre inside you, who can die?
How is death possible?
Death is possible to the ego, to the self.
How can death happen to the no-self?
All the enlightened people through the ages
have been saying only one thing:
Die to the ego so that you can attain to the eternal.
Let the ego die,
then there will be no death for you, you become deathless.

A Field Dyed Deep Violet
28th February 1975

Ninagawa-Shinzaemon, a linked-verse poet, and devotee of Zen,
desired to become a disciple of the remarkable master, Ikkyu,
who was Abbot of the Daitokuji in Murasakino—a violet field.

He called upon Ikkyu,
and the following dialogue took place at the temple entrance.

Ikkyu: Who are you?
Ninagawa: A devotee of Buddhism.
Ikkyu: You are from?
Ninagawa: Your region.
Ikkyu: Ah. And what's happening there these days?
Ninagawa: The crows caw, the sparrows twitter.
Ikkyu: And where do you think you are now?
Ninagawa: In a field dyed deep violet.
Ikkyu: Why?
Ninagawa: Miscanthus, morning glories,
safflowers, chrysanthemums, asters.
Ikkyu: And after they're gone?
Ninagawa: It is Miyagino—the field of autumn flowering.
Ikkyu: What happens in that field?
Ninagawa: The stream flows through, the wind sweeps over.

Amazed at Ninagawa's Zen-like speech,
Ikkyu led him to his room and served him tea.
Then he spoke this impromptu verse:

I want to serve
you delicacies.
Alas! the Zen sect
can offer nothing.

At which the visitor replied:

The mind which treats me
to nothing is the original void—
a delicacy of delicacies.

Deeply moved, the master said:
My son, you have learned much.

Poetry is closer than theology to religion,
imagination nearer than reason.
And, of course, religion transcends both—it is neither.

But through logic, to drop into the abyss of religion
is a little bit difficult,
because logic has a rigidity about it.
It is not flexible; it is closed, not open;
it has no windows, no doors, to go out of itself.
It is like a grave.
One can die within it,
but one cannot move into a living process,
one cannot become more alive through it.
Logic is a straitjacket, a prison.

Poetry is closer to religion,
because it is more flexible, liquid, more flowing.
It is not religion,
but you can drop out of it more easily than from logic.
It has openings—doors and windows—
and fresh winds can always reach into the deepest core
of the heart of a poet.
Poetry is not rigid; you can drop out of it, if you like;
it will not cling to you.
And, because it is imaginative,
it can stumble, even unknowingly, upon the unknown.
It goes on groping in the dark—it *is* a groping in the dark—
and it goes on groping, it goes on searching.
It is always ready to move into any new dimension.

Logic is resistant:
you cannot find more orthodox people than logicians.
They will never listen to a new dimension opening,
they will not even look at it.
They will simply say it is not possible.
All that is possible, they think, is already known;
all that can happen has already happened.
They are always suspicious of the unknown.

The heart of the poet is always in love with the unknown.
He goes on groping in the dark for something new,
something original, something untasted before,
something unlived, unexperienced.
A poet gropes.
And sometimes he can stumble upon the unknown,
he can fall into the abyss of religion.

Poetry is metaphoric, metaphorical, it lives through metaphors.
The same is the language of religion.
Of course, when a metaphor is used in a poetic way,
it means one thing;
and when it is used in a religious way,
it means something else.
But both use metaphors. There is a meeting ground.
Their meanings may differ, but their methods
are of the same family. They look like twins.
Vast is the difference within, but at least in form,
at the surface, they are more alike than logic and religion.

Because of this likeness
religion has always spoken in the way of the poet:
Upanishads, Vedas, Kabir, Meera, Zen poets. . . .

Zen poets have written beautiful haikus, so condensed
that a vast poetic world becomes like a seed in the haiku.
Sometimes they are very simple,
you cannot even catch the significance immediately.
But if you ponder over them, meditate upon them,
then, by and by, the small haiku becomes a door.
A few days before I was reading Basho's famous haiku.
It is very small,
but if you meditate upon it, suddenly a door opens.
The haiku is:
'Old pond
frog jump-in
water-sound'
Just visualise it—
an old pond, very ancient, a frog jumps in, the water-sound.
Finished. Nothing more to say. A whole situation condensed.
If you meditate on it,
suddenly you will feel a silence surrounding you.
Something will change within you.
It is objective art.

Zen poets, Sufi mystics, Hindu saints,
have all spoken in the language of poetry,
and even if sometimes Buddha and Mahavir and Jesus
don't speak in the language of poetry,
the poetry is still there, whether they speak in it or not.
If you listen to them, you will feel a certain poetic quality
underneath their words. Their prose is only on the surface.
The form is of prose, but the spirit is of poetry.
In fact, one who is enlightened cannot do otherwise.
If he must speak in prose, he can; but he cannot avoid poetry.
The poetry will be there just beneath the surface—
if you have a little insight, you will see it;
it is vibrant and alive there.
Religion and poetry have the same language:
their words differ, but somewhere they have a meeting point.
And that meeting point is the subject of this story.

A poet comes to meet a Zen master.
He must have been a very great poet,
because only the highest and greatest poets
can have a meeting ground with the mystic.
Each and every poet will not have that,
because where the poetry becomes ultimate,
there is the first step of mysticism.
Where the poetry ends, culminates,
reaches its peak, its *Gourishankar,* becomes the Everest,
there is the first step of the temple of the mystic.
The highest poetry is the lowest mysticism—
there is the meeting point.
So only very great poets can attain to the height
where a Zen master will have to say:
My son, you have learned much.

Now we should enter into this story.

Ninagawa-Shinzaemon, a linked-verse poet, and devotee of Zen, desired to become a disciple of the remarkable master, Ikkyu, who was Abbot of the Daitokuji in Murasakino—a violet field.

This has always been my feeling:
that the greatest of the poets cannot avoid religion;
they have to come into it,
because poetry leads to a certain point,
and beyond that is religion.
If you persist in being a poet, you will become religious.
You can remain a poet only if you have not travelled
the whole extent of it.
So only small poets can remain poets:
great poets are bound to move into religion.
You cannot escape it, because a certain point comes
where the poetry ends and religion begins.
If you follow up to that extent, where will you go?
At that moment poetry converts itself into religion.
One has to follow.

The same thing happens to a logician, to a scientist,
but in a different way.
With a scientist also, if he persists, goes on and on and on,
there comes a moment
where he feels there is a cul-de-sac, the road moves nowhere.
Now there comes an abyss, there is no more road ahead.

A Field Dyed Deep Violet

It is different with a poet:
there is a road ahead, but now it is no longer of poetry.
His road automatically converts into the road of religion.
But for a scientist, a logician, or a philosopher,
it happens in a different way.
He comes to a cul-de-sac, the road simply ends.
It goes no further, there is no road,
just a precipice, an abyss.

This happened to Albert Einstein in his last days.
It can happen only to the greatest. The lesser minds
on the same road never reach to the cul-de-sac point.
They die somewhere on the road
believing that the road was leading somewhere,
because there was still road ahead of them.
The conversion happens only to the greatest.
In the last days of Albert Einstein's life,
he started feeling that his whole life had been a wastage.
Somebody asked him:
If you are born again, what would you like to be?
He said: Never again a scientist.
I would rather be a plumber,
but never again a scientist. Finished!
In the last days, he started thinking about God,
or the ultimate meaning of life, the mystery of mysteries,
and he said: The more I penetrated
into the mystery of existence, the more and more I felt
that tne mystery is eternal, unending, infinite.
The more I came to know,
the less I became certain about my knowledge.

The mystery is vast, it cannot be exhausted.
This is what a concept of God is:
the mysterious, the vast, that which cannot be exhausted.
You can know, and know, and know,
and still it remains unknown.
You move into it, and go in, and in, and in,
and still you are moving on the periphery.
You go on dropping into it, but there is no bottom to it.
You can never exactly reach to the centre of the mystery.
The moment never comes when you can say: I have known all.
Nobody has said that, except focis.
A wise man starts feeling more and more ignorant,

only fools gather a few things from here and there,
and start thinking that they know.
Only fools are knowers, claimers of knowledge.

Even in a scientific search
the moment comes when the road leads nowhere.
Then, suddenly, there is a jump.
A poet can move into religion without any jump,
he can simply slip, the roads are linked together.
But a scientist has to take a jump:
a total about-turn, three hundred and sixty degrees.
He has to go completely upside down, inside out, outside in.
But a poet can simply slip,
like a snake slipping out of his old skin.
That's why I say that poetry is closer to religion.

This man, Ninagawa, must have been a very, very great poet;
hence he became interested in Zen, meditation.

If poetry does not lead you to meditation, it is not poetry.
At the most, it may be a clever composition of words,
but there will be no poetry in it.
You may be a good linguist, a good composer, a good grammarian,
one who knows all the rules about how to write poetry,
but you are not a poet—
because poetry in its deepest core is meditative.

A poet is not a composer: a poet is a visionary.
He doesn't compose,
the poetry happens to him in certain moments—
those moments are of meditation.
In fact, when the poet is not, then the poetry happens.
When the poet is completely absent,
suddenly he is filled with something unknown, unasked for;
suddenly something of the unknown has entered into him,
a fresh breeze has come into his house.
Now he has to translate this fresh breeze into language—
he is not a composer, he is a translator.
A poet is a translator: something happens inside his being
and he translates it into language, into words.
Something wordless stirs within.
It is more like a feeling, and less like a thought.
It is less in the head, and more in the heart.

A poet is very courageous.
To live with the heart takes the deepest courage.
The word 'courage' is very interesting.
It comes from a latin root 'cor', which means the heart.
The word courage comes from the root 'cor'.
Cor means the heart—
so to be courageous means to live with the heart.
And weaklings, only weaklings, live with the head;
afraid, they created a security of logic around them;
fearful, they close every window and door
with theology, concepts, words, theories—
and inside them they hide.

The way of the heart is the way of courage.
It is to live in insecurity;
it is to live in love, and trust;
it is to move in the unknown;
it is leaving the past and allowing the future to be.
Courage is to move on dangerous paths:
life is dangerou· and only cowards can avoid the danger.
But then, they are already dead.
A person who is alive, really alive, vitally alive,
will always move into the unknown.
There is danger there, but he will take the risk.
The heart is always ready to take the risk,
the heart is a gambler, the head is a businessman.
The head always calculates—it is cunning.
The heart is non-calculating.

This English word 'courage' is beautiful, very interesting.
To live through the heart is the meaning:
a poet lives through the heart.
And, by and by, in the heart
he starts listening to the sounds of the unknown.
The head cannot listen; it is very far away from the unknown.
The head is filled with the known.

What is your mind? It is all that you have known.
It is the past, the dead, that which has gone.
Mind is nothing but the accumulated past, the memory.
Heart is the future, heart is always the hope,
heart is always somewhere in the future.
Head thinks about the past; heart dreams about the future.

And I tell you
that the present is nearer to the future than to the past.
That's why I say that the poet is nearer to religion.
Philosophy, logic, metaphysics, theology, science,
all belong to the past, the known;
poetry, music, dance, art—all the arts—belong to the future.

Religion belongs to the present,
and I tell you that the future is nearer to the present
than to the past, because the past is already gone.
The future is to come. The future is yet to be.
The future has yet the possibility.
It will come; it is already coming.
Every moment it is becoming the present,
every moment the future is becoming the present,
and the present is becoming the past.
The past has no possibility, it has been used.
You have already moved away from it—it is exhausted,
it is a dead thing, it is like a grave.
The future is like a seed; it is coming, ever coming,
always reaching and meeting with the present.
You are always moving.
The present is nothing but a movement into the future;
it is already the step that you have taken;
it is going into the future.
Poetry is concerned with possibility, hope, dreams;
it is nearer.

This man, Ninagawa, must have been a great poet.
Why do I say he must have been a great poet?—
I have not read his poetry, I don't know what he wrote.
But I say he must have been a great poet,
because he became interested in Zen.
And not only that—he
desired to become a disciple of the remarkable master, Ikkyu.

To be interested in Zen is not enough
unless you become a disciple.
To be interested in religion is not enough—
it is good, but it doesn't go very far.
Interest remains a curiosity, interest remains mental,
unless you take a jump into commitment,
unless you become a disciple.

A Field Dyed Deep Violet

To become a disciple is a great decision.
It is no ordinary decision,
it is a very difficult, almost impossible decision.
I always say that to become a disciple
is the most impossible revolution.
Because how can one trust another?
How can one leave his life in the hands of another?
It is the most impossible revolution, but it happens,
and when it happens, it is beautiful, there is nothing like it.
But only those who are very courageous, almost daredevils,
only they can take the step. It is not for cowards.
It is not for head-oriented people.
It is for those who live in the heart,
for those who have courage, for those who can risk.
This is the greatest gamble ever
because you risk your total life,
you give yourself to somebody.
You don't know who he is, you cannot know.
You may feel certain things,
but you can never be certain about the master.
Always a doubt remains.
In spite of the doubt, one has to take the jump.
The doubt cannot be satisfied. No.
You can hide it, but you cannot convince the doubting part—
how can you convince it?
You have to be with the master,
only then will the doubt disappear. Before it is not possible.
Only experience will help it to disappear.
So how can you convince it?

The mind always hesitates.
People come to me and they say that they are hesitating,
they are fifty-fifty, what to do? Should they wait?
If they wait, they can wait for ever,
because if they think that they will take the jump
only when the mind is a hundred per cent certain, convinced,
then they will never take it.
Because the mind can never be a hundred per cent for something—
that is the nature of the mind.
It is always divided, fragmented; it can never be total.
That is the difference between heart and mind.
Heart is always total, mind is always divided.
Mind is the division of your being:

heart is the undivided being.

Discipleship is of the heart.
The mind goes on rambling and talking
and doubting and being suspicious. In spite of that,
in spite of the chattering mind, one takes the jump.
I say 'in spite of that'. That is the only way—
you simply don't listen to the mind.
You simply move beneath the mind,
reach the heart, and ask the heart.
Discipleship is like love,
it is not like a business partnership. It is not a bargain.
You simply give,
without knowing whether something is going to happen or not.
Whether you will receive anything back, you don't know.
You simply give.
That's why it is courage.

He was not only interested in Zen, he was a devotee.
He loved it.
Interest, curiosity, enquiry, is of the mind,
devotion is of the heart.

. . .*desired to become a disciple.*
What is becoming a disciple? What does it mean? It means:
I have tried, and failed; I have searched and couldn't find;
I have done all that I could do, and I have remained the same.
No transformation has happened to me.
So I surrender.
Now, the master will be the deciding factor, not me.
I will simply follow him like a shadow.
Whatsoever he says I will do. I will not ask for proofs.
I will not ask that he should first convince me.
I will not argue, I will simply follow—
in deep trust.

The mind may still go on about:
What are you doing? This is not good.
This will not lead anywhere, this is foolish, this is mad.
The mind will go on saying this,
but, once you have taken the decision to be a disciple,
you don't listen to the mind, you listen to the master.
Up to now you have listened to your own mind, the ego,
from now onwards, you will listen to the master,

now the master will be your mind.
This is the meaning of discipleship:
you will put yourself aside and allow the master
to penetrate into the deepest core of your being.
You are no more. Now only the master is.
To be a disciple means to be a shadow,
to put your ego completely aside.

*He called upon Ikkyu,
and the following dialogue took place at the temple entrance.*

Zen stories are very, very meaningful:
no word is there unnecessarily, not even a single word.

. . .the following dialogue took place at the temple entrance.
First, the word 'dialogue'.
Dialogue is not just talking, it is not discussing,
it is not arguing, it is not a debate.
A dialogue has a different quality.
A dialogue is the meeting of two beings,
meeting in love, trying to understand each other.
Not trying to argue, not trying to discuss—
just a very sympathetic attitude.
Dialogue is participating in the being of the other:
two friends or two lovers talking with no antagonism inside,
with no effort to prove yourself right, and the other wrong.

That happens while you are talking with people—
you go on and on in subtle ways,
trying to prove that you are right.
And the other goes on trying to prove that he is right.
Then dialogue is not possible. Dialogue means
trying to understand the other with an open mind.
Dialogue is a rare phenomenon and it is beautiful,
because both are enriched through a dialogue.
In fact, while you talk, either it can be a discussion
—both opposite to each other, a verbal fight,
trying to prove that I am right and you are wrong—
or a dialogue, which is different.
Dialogue is not posing against each other,
but taking each other's hand,
moving together towards the truth,
helping each other to find the way.

It is togetherness, it is a co-operation,
it is a harmonious effort to find the truth.
It is not in any way a fight, not at all.
It is a friendship, moving together to find the truth,
helping each other to find the truth.
Nobody has the truth already, but when two persons
start finding out, enquiring about the truth together,
that is dialogue—and both are enriched.
And when truth is found, it is neither of me, nor of you.
When truth is found,
it is greater than both who participated in the enquiry,
it is higher than both, it surrounds both—
and both are enriched.

Dialogue is the beginning between a master and a disciple;
and it must happen at the entrance,
otherwise going into the temple is not possible.
Hence the words 'at the entrance'—it must happen at the gate.
The first thing is the dialogue: if it doesn't happen,
then there is no possibility of any disciplehood.
Then Ikkyu would have said good-bye, at the very entrance,
because there would be no need to invite the person
into the temple, there would be no meaning in it.
So sitting at the entrance, just sitting on the steps,
this dialogue happened.

Ikkyu tried to feel the man.
He had to feel the man,
the potentiality, the possibility, the attitude.
How deep was the enquiry? How deep was the urge to enquire?
Was it just a curiosity?
Was he just a philosopher, or really a devotee?
Ikkyu was just trying to feel his being,
and Ninagawa allowed it, he participated in it.
He didn't become scared, he didn't try to defend,
he didn't try to pretend to be something which he was not.
He opened his heart to this man completely.
He allowed this man to enter in him, to feel,
because that's how a master has to decide whether
you have come here accidentally, or you have really come.

The coming can be accidental—
somebody told you and you were passing by the road

A Field Dyed Deep Violet

so you said: Okay, there is time enough to go to the movie.
Let us go and see who this master is.

If it is accidental
then it is better to end the relationship at the entrance,
because it will lead nowhere.
If the mind is argumentative,
if the mind is too filled with its own ideas,
then you can become a student, but not a disciple.
And a master is not a teacher,
he is not in search of students, he is not running a school.
He is creating a temple of the heart, he is making a shrine;
he is bringing a holy, sacred phenomenon to the earth.

Ikkyu had to feel, and he felt him very deeply,
and the man proved his mettle, he was authentic.
He didn't react, he responded to the master,
and whatsoever the master asked, he gave a total response to it.
Those responses are beautiful, move slowly.

He called upon Ikkyu,
and the following dialogue took place at the temple entrance.
Ikkyu: Who are you?

That is going to be the whole search.
'Who am I?' is all that religion is about.
If you already know who you are,
then there is no need to bother.
Or, if in your ignorance
you have become identified with the name and the form,
too identified, too filled with your name and form,
then, too, you are not yet mature enough
for a master like Ikkyu to accept you.
You have to go to a lesser master,
in fact, to a teacher who will teach you
that you are not the name, and you are not the form,
and you are not the body, and this and that,
and create a philosophical soil
into which a master can throw the seed.
You need to go to some teacher.
So the first thing Ikkyu asked was: Who are you?

Ninagawa said: A devotee of Buddhism.
A very, very humble attitude—non-claiming.

He didn't say his name, that: I am Ninagawa—you don't know?
Have you not heard about the greatest poet in the country?
Don't you read newspapers?
What nonsense are you asking: Who are you?
Everybody knows in the country, even the emperor.

Poets are very, very egoistical people.
Poets, writers, novelists—all have very crystallised egos.
You cannot find more egoistical people than literary people.
It is very difficult to have any dialogue with them.
They already know.
They can teach you, but they cannot be taught.
Just because they can compose a few lines,
just because they can write an article, or a novel, or a story,
they start feeling very much that they are somebodies.
In fact, a real poet will have no ego—
if a poet has a very crystallised ego, he is not a poet at all.
Because he has learned nothing out of his poetry,
he has not even learned this basic truth:
that poetry descends only when you are not.
So he must be composing, he must be doing something.
Poetry can be a technique, so he may be a technician,
but he is not a poet.
He may be able to arrange beautiful words, in rhythm,
he may follow all the rules, he may be perfect—
but he is not a poet.
He may be clever, technically right,
but deep inside, if the ego is still there,
he does not know what poetry is,
because poetry happens only when you are not.
In fact, a great poet will not claim
that he is the creator of this poetry.
How can he claim it? He was not when it happened.

It happened that when Coleridge—one of the greatest poets—
died, he left almost forty thousand pieces incomplete.
He would start a poem, write three lines, and then stop.
Years would pass, and then suddenly one day
he would add two more lines, then stop.
Forty thousand incomplete poems!
Just before he died, somebody asked: What have you been doing?
These are such beautiful things, why don't you complete them?
He said: How can I complete them?

I never wrote them, they came. When they come, they come;
when they don't come, they don't come. What can I do?
They cannot be pulled, they cannot be forced to come.
I don't know from where they come:
out of the blue a line descends.
Sometimes the whole poem comes in succession,
sometimes not, and nothing can be done
because I don't know from where they come.
In fact, when they come I am not.
I am so dazed, I become just a void.
So how can I complete them?

That's why ancient poems exist without any signature.
Nobody knows who wrote them.
Who wrote the Upanishads, the greatest of poems—
who wrote them, nobody knows.
The authors never signed them,
they never signed them because they felt so humble.
They were not the makers, not the creators.

When Ninagawa was asked, 'Who are you?'
if he had been just like other poets, ordinary poets
and writers and authors, too filled with their own egos,
he would have said something like:
You don't know that I am a Nobel Laureate, a Nobel Prize winner,
and that the emperor has praised me
and appointed me as the royal poet?
No. Ninagawa said: *A devotee of Buddhism.*
He didn't talk about poetry,
he didn't talk about his famous name,
he didn't talk about himself at all.
He simply said: *A devotee of Buddhism*—a devotee of Buddha.
A devotee—that showed that he was there
because of his heart, because of his love.
He was there not because of his reasoning,
he was there because of his feeling. Just a devotee.

Ikkyu: You are from?
Ninagawa: Your region.

A beautiful metaphor.
In fact he was from the region,
from the same part of the country, from where Ikkyu came.

But he was not talking about that.
He was talking about the inner region, the inner search:
Maybe you are far ahead,
maybe you have reached, and I am just a beginner,
but I belong to the same region, the search is the same.
I am a fellow traveller.
Once your heart is filled with the urge to know the truth,
you become a fellow traveller of all the Buddhas.
They have reached: you will reach.
Maybe it will take many, many lives,
but that makes no difference—you have started on the path.
You may be just at the beginning,
but now you are a fellow traveller.

Says Ninagawa: *Your region.*
I belong to the same part of the world to which you belong.
Ikkyu: Ah. And what's happening there these days?
He goes on poking at him, provoking him,
maybe he is just a pretender trying to deceive,
saying beautiful things learned somewhere, borrowed.
He may have been a scholar of Zen classics
where such dialogues are given. But he cannot escape Ikkyu.
If he is a pretender, he will fall somewhere or other.

Ah. And what's happening there these days?
Ikkyu brings him back and back.
He understands what Ninagawa is saying,
what he means by 'your region',
but he doesn't allow it for a moment.
So he says: What is happening there these days?
Who has become the prime minister there?
Whose wife has moved with whom?
Some rumour, some gossip; what is happening there?
Some events must have taken place—
somebody died, somebody got married.
Events—what is happening there?

Ninagawa: The crows caw, the sparrows twitter.
Prime ministers, ministers, and their world,
politics, the market, economics, are not real history.
They are just accidents; they happen on the periphery.
They are not part of eternity, they happen in time.
What is eternal is the only news for those who know,

A Field Dyed Deep Violet

and what is accidental is the only news
for those who don't know.

Ninagawa: The crows caw, the sparrows twitter.
This is the eternal news, which has always been happening
and is happening still.
Summer and winter, nature flows, and clouds come and go.
This is eternity.
In the morning the sun rises, and in the evening the sun sets,
still.
And in the night there are stars in the sky
with their subtle music.
This is all.
That is the real news.
The crows don't bother who has become the prime minister,
and the sparrows don't pay a single, a single bit of attention
to the world of events.
Only man is filled with this junk.

Henry Ford has said: History is bunk.
It is rare for something like this to come from a very rich man,
but it is true.
What does it matter whether Napoleon wins or is defeated?
Who rules? The eternal moves,
not even aware that these things are happening.
What is Ninagawa saying? He is saying it is always the same;
The crows caw, the sparrows twitter.

And where do you think you are now?
Ikkyu's hard—from another dimension he attacks.
And where do you think you are now?
Ninagawa: In a field dyed deep violet.
The temple was known as the violet field, Murasakino.
Ikkyu: Why?
Why do you call it that?
You are in a field dyed deep violet.
Why do you call it *dyed deep violet?*
Ninagawa: Miscanthus, morning glories,
 safflowers, chrysanthemums, asters.

Flowers all over.
Ninagawa doesn't say that this was the name of the temple—
violet field.

Names belong to the memory, to the past,
and the master was asking about the now.
And now, all over, all around are flowers:
Miscanthus, morning glories,
safflowers, chysanthemums, asters.
They were giving the whole place a deep violet colour.
When Ikkyu asked about the now, Ninagawa talked about the now.

Ikkyu is really impossible; he won't relax. He asks:
And after they're gone?
These flowers are here now, okay,
so you call it a deep violet colour, a violet field.
But soon these flowers will be gone,
then what will you call it, after they are gone?
Ninagawa: It is Miyagino—the field of autumn flowering.

This is to be understood.
Clouds come and go—these are two aspects of the same coin.
Flowers flower, then disappear—
these are also two aspects of the same phenomenon.
Absence and presence are not opposite:
they are two aspects of the same thing.
Now there are flowers, so it is called the violet field,
and when the flowers are gone people will say
that this is the field of the absence of these autumn flowers.
It will still be the violet field,
but from the other side, the absence.

It happened once that a Zen master loved his mother very much.
In fact, before he became a Zen disciple, his father died.
He wanted to become a Zen monk, but his mother said:
I am poor, and I am alone, and your father is dead.
So he said: Don't worry. Even when I become a monk,
I will be your son and you will be my mother.
I am not renouncing, you are not losing anything.
So the mother allowed him to become a monk.

He loved the mother very much. He would go to the market
to purchase things for her, and people would laugh.
They would say: We have never seen a monk purchasing things.
Buddhist monks simply beg; and not only would he not be begging,
he would be purchasing meat and fish,
and people would simply ridicule him. This was too much.

A Field Dyed Deep Violet

Of course, he was buying these things for his mother,
not for himself;
she liked them and she was not a nun or a religious person.
Then the mother, seeing that people laughed,
that the whole town laughed about a monk purchasing fish,
became a vegetarian.
And because people laughed about him purchasing things,
she said: Don't go. I will purchase them myself.
He continued to be a devoted son.

Then one day he went to preach somewhere
and the mother died when he was not there.
He came just in time; the dead body was there
and people were getting ready to take it to the cemetery.
He came near the body and said: Mother, so you have left?
And he himself replied: Yes, son, I have left the body.
Then he said: Don't be too worried,
because soon I will also be leaving the body.
Then he replied, from the mother's side:
Good, I will wait for you.
And then he told the people:
I have said good-bye to my mother. The dialogue is over.
The funeral is over. Now you can take the dead body.
Somebody asked: We cannot follow, what is the matter?
To whom were you talking?
He said: To the absence of my mother,
because that is another aspect of her being.
They asked: But why were you answering?
He said: Because she could not answer, so I had to do both.
Absence cannot answer, so I had to answer from her side.
But she is there, as she was before,
only now she is in her absent aspect.

So when Ikkyu asked: *And after they are gone?*
Ninagawa said: *It is Miyagino—the field of autumn flowering.*
It is the same field, but in an absent aspect.
Manifested or unmanifested, being or non-being,
life or death, are two aspects of the same phenomenon.
There is nothing to choose, and those who choose are stupid,
and unnecessarily fall into suffering.
Now amazed, Ikkyu asked the last question:
What happens in that field—when flowers are gone?
Ninagawa: *The stream flows through, the wind sweeps over.*

Amazed at Ninagawa's Zen-like speech, Ikkyu led him to his room
and served him tea.

Remember, it is Zen-like, but it is not exactly Zen.
He is a poet, and a very great poet of deep understanding,
but the highest of poetry is just the beginning of Zen,
the beginning of religion.

It is Zen-like stuff.
He understands, he has a certain glimpse,
he is open, he feels,
he has groped in the dark and he knows a certain quality;
through his own enquiry he has stumbled upon it.
But still it is just a glimpse.
Sometimes it can happen—
a dark night, a sudden lightning, and you have a glimpse.
Then again there is darkness.
This is what happens to the greatest poet:
he is just on the boundary line
from where he can have glimpses of the beyond.
But they are glimpses. They are Zen-like.

When will they become Zen?
They will become Zen only when they are no longer glimpses,
but have become your very being.
Then you live in them from moment to moment,
they don't come and go.
They have simply become your innermost being, the way you are.
It is not like lightning, it is full noontide, it is day;
the sun is high in the sky and remains there;
there is no possibility of darkness coming again.
It is not a glimpse, it has become part of you,
you carry it wherever you go.
The inner light is burning now—
you don't depend on accidents, you have settled in it,
it has become your home.

Trying to reach reality through the head
is just like someone trying to see through the ears.
It is not possible. Ears can hear, but cannot see.
Trying to reach reality through the heart
is like trying to see with the hands.
The hands cannot see,
but they can still give a glimpse of what seeing can be.

A blind person, if he loves a woman,
touches her face, feels the curves, touches the body,
feels the roundness, the warmth and the marble-like texture,
then through the hands comes a certain glimpse of seeing.
Hands can give you a certain glimpse of seeing,
not exactly seeing because how can hands see?
They can only grope.
But when you touch a face with closed eyes,
you can feel the curves,
the nose, the eyes, the way the face is.

A poet is like a hand,
he feels the nature of reality with his hands.
Certain glimpses come to him, Zen-like.
And a real man of Zen is like eyes,
he is not groping, he has no need to touch with the hand—
he can see.

Amazed at Ninagawa's Zen-like speech, Ikkyu led him to his room and served him tea.
These are symbols showing that you are allowed—
come nearer and closer.

...and served him tea.
Tea is a Zen symbol which means awareness,
because tea makes you more alert, more aware.
Tea was invented by Buddhists
and for centuries they have used tea as a help in meditation.
And tea is helpful.
If you take a cup of tea, strong, and then sit in meditation
for at least one hour you will not feel sleepy,
and you can remain aware.
Otherwise, whenever you feel silent, and sit relaxed,
sleep comes. To avoid sleep, tea has helped.

The story is that Bodhidharma
was meditating on a certain mountain in China called 'Ta'.
From that 'Ta' comes the name 'tea'.
That mountain can be pronounced as 'Ta', or 'Cha';
that's why in India tea is called 'chai', or 'cha'.

Bodhidharma was meditating, he was really a great meditator.
He liked to meditate for eighteen hours, but it was difficult.
He would feel sleepy again and again,

and his eyelids would drop, again and again.
So he cut off his eyelids and threw them away,
now there was no possibility of closing the eyes.
The story is beautiful—
those eyelids became the first seeds of tea,
and a certain plant came out of them.
Bodhidharma prepared the first tea in the world
out of the plants, and he was amazed to find
that if you took the leaves and drank them,
you could remain alert for longer periods.
So for centuries Zen people have been drinking tea,
and tea has become a very, very sacred thing.

When a Zen master serves tea, it is a metaphor.
He is saying: Be more aware.
You are on the right path, he says to Ninagawa,
you are on the right path, but you are walking a little sleepily.
You have found the direction, now move in the same direction.
Soon your Zen-like being will become Zen,
but you will need to be more aware.
Amazed at Ninagawa's Zen-like speech, Ikkyu led him to his room and served him tea.
He is serving awareness, a cup full of awareness.
It is a symbol to indicate that he should become more aware,
that's all that he needs.

Then Ikkyu spoke this impromptu verse:
I want to serve
you delicacies.
Alas! the Zen sect
can offer nothing.

It has two meanings.
The ordinary meaning is that
in the Zen sect delicacies are not allowed.
Very simple food is allowed;
rice, a few vegetables, tea—no delicacies.
So the first, the ordinary meaning is:
I want to serve
you delicacies.
Alas! the Zen sect
can offer nothing.
This is the last effort of Ikkyu

to penetrate him to the deepest core,
to see whether he can understand the meaning or not.

The second meaning is:
*I want to serve
you delicacies.
Alas! the Zen sect
can offer...
only nothing.*
I can offer nothing.
It can mean: I cannot offer anything,
or it can mean: I can offer you only nothing.
Then nothing is offered.
Awareness and nothingness are two aspects of the same thing.
The more you become aware, the more you feel being nothing.

So first Ikkyu served tea to say: Become aware.
Then he says: Alas! I cannot offer anything—except nothing.

This is the last net thrown by the master.
After he had given the tea,
if Ninagawa had been a pretender, he would have relaxed.
He would have thought:
I am accepted. The master has led me to his tea-room,
offered me tea, served me tea. I am relaxed.
After taking tea he would have relaxed,
because you cannot pretend for long.
Pretension is such a strain that one relaxes.
And when the master has served and given you tea,
now there is no need to pretend, everything is finished.
So it was the last trap.

Ninagawa replied:
*The mind which treats me
to nothing is the original void—
a delicacy of delicacies.*
No. He had a really Zen-like understanding,
he was not a mere poet.
Something of the real poetry of existence had happened to him.
He could immediately understand.
He could be immediate and he could respond.
He said:
*The mind which treats me
to nothing is the original void—*

a delicacy of delicacies.
Nothing is the delicacy of delicacies—
more than that cannot be offered.
That is the last delicacy, the last taste of existence itself.
It is as if you have eaten God himself—
the delicacy of delicacies.

Deeply moved, the master said:
My son, you have learned much.

This learning is not knowledge.
Zen makes a difference between learning and knowledge,
let me explain it to you.
Knowledge is borrowed: learning is yours.
Knowledge is through words, language, concepts:
learning is through experience.
Knowledge is always finished: you know it, it is complete.
Learning is never complete, it is always on the way.
Learning is a process—one goes on and on and on,
to the very last moment one goes on learning.
Knowledge stops somewhere, and becomes the ego.
Learning never stops, it remains humbleness.
Knowledge is borrowed:
you cannot deceive a master by your knowledge,
because your words will be just on the surface;
deep down your being will show. Your words cannot hide you.
For a master your words are transparent.
Whatsoever you show that you know
he can always see behind to what is really there.
This man would have been caught by Ikkyu
if he had been a man of knowledge.
But no, he was really a man of learning:
he had learned, he was not pretending.
Through many experiences of life, existence, he had learned much.
My son, said Ikkyu, you have learned much.

And this is very much from a Zen master,
because they are very miserly about saying such things.
When a Zen master says such a thing he means it.
And he can say such a thing only when he is really moved,
when he really feels the authentic.
Only then, otherwise not.

Look into this story, and feel yourself parallel to it.
Have you learned, or have you only gathered knowledge?
Let it become a very fundamental law:
don't react through knowledge,
react—that is, respond—spontaneously.
Only then will you be closer and closer to me,
and only then, one day, can I lead you in and serve you tea.
Otherwise you can just be physically closer to me
and that won't help.
I have to serve awareness to you
and I have to give you the delicacy of delicacies—
nothingness.

by bhagwan shree rajneesh

- The Ultimate Alchemy   Vols I and II
  (discourses on the Atma Pooja Upanishad)

- The Book of the Secrets   Vols I, II, III and IV
  (discourses on Tantra)

- The Supreme Doctrine
  (discourses on the Kenopanishad)

- YOGA: the alpha and the omega   Vols I, II, and III
  (discourses on Patanjali's Yoga Sutras)

- VEDANTA: Seven Steps to Samadhi
  (discourses on the Akshya Upanishad)

- The Way of the White Cloud
  (talks based on questions)

- Roots and Wings
  (talks based on questions)

- The Empty Boat
  (discourses on Chuang Tzu)

- No Water, No Moon
  (discourses on Zen)

- The Mustard Seed   Vols I and II
  (discourses on the sayings of Jesus)

- When the Shoe Fits
  (discourses on Chuang Tzu)

- Neither This Nor That
  (discourses on Sosan—Zen)

- ...and the flowers showered
  (discourses on Zen stories)

- Returning to the Source
  (discourses on Zen stories)

- The Hidden Harmony
  (discourses on the fragments of Heraclitus)

- TANTRA: The Supreme Understanding
  (discourses on Tilopa's Song of Mahamudra)

- The Grass Grows by Itself
  (discourses on Zen stories)

- Until You Die
  (discourses on Sufi stories)

- Just Like That
  (discourses on Sufi Stories)

- TAO: The Three Treasures   Vols I and II
  (discourses on Lao Tzu)

- Hammer on the Rock
  (darshan interviews)

- Come Follow Me   Vol I
  (discourses on the life of Jesus)

- I am the Gate
  (talks based on questions)

- The Silent Explosion
  (talks based on questions)

- Dimensions beyond the Known
  (talks based on questions)

translations

- La Rivoluzione Interiore
  (Italian—published by Armenia Editore)

- Hu Meditation og Kosmic Orgasme
  (Danish—published by Borgens Forlag A/S)

rajneesh meditation centres

- SHREE RAJNEESH ASHRAM, 17 Koregaon Park, Poona 411 001, India
  Tel: 28127

- SAGAR DEEP, 52 Ridge Road, Malabar Hill, Bombay 400 006, India
  Tel: 364783

- ANANDA, 29 East 28th St., N.Y.C. 10016, USA
  Tel: 212 686-3261

- NEELAMBER, Blackmore Lane, P.O.Box 143 East Islip, N.Y.11730, USA
  Tel: 516 581-0004

- ANAND TARU, 12, Hearn St., Watertown, Boston, Mass., USA

- BODHITARU, 7231 SW 62nd Place, Miami, Florida, USA

- SATSANG, 887 North La Salle, Chicago, Illinois, USA
  Tel: 312 943-8561/8549

- PARAS, P.O.Box 22174, San Francisco, Calif 94122, USA
  Tel: 415 664-6600

- ARVIND, 1330 Renfrew St., Vancouver, B.C., Canada

- KALPTARU, Top Floor, 10a Belmont Street, London NW1, England
  (Postal Address: 28 Oak Village, London NW5)   Tel: 267-8304

- NIRVANA, 82 Bell St., London NW1, England   Tel: 262-0991

- SURYODAYA, The Old Rectory, Gislingham, by Diss, nr Eye, Suffolk, England

- GOURISHANKER, 153 Dalkeith Road, Edinburgh, Scotland
  Tel: 031 667-2833

- PRASTHAN, 21 Wilmot Road, Glasgow C13 1XL, Scotland

- PREMPATH, 45-390 Desmonts, France

- SHANTIDWEEP, 25 Avenue Pierre, Premier de Serbie, Paris XVIe, France
  Tel: 700-7930

- ANAND NIKETAN, Kobmagergade 43.1150, Copenhagen K, Denmark

- ARIHANT, Via Cacciatori delle Alpi 19, 20019 Settimo Milanese,
  Milan, Italy

- SATYAM, 15B Route de Loëx, 1213 Onex, Geneva, Switzerland
  Tel: 022 93-19-46

- AMITABH, Korte Prinsengracht 9, Amsterdam, Holland
  Tel: 238966

- PURVODAYA, D-8051 Margaretenreid, Munich, West Germany

- SHREYAS, 8 Munich 60, Raucheneggerstr. 11, West Germany
  Tel: 809 882662

- ANANDLOK, 1, Berlin 61, Luckenwaldstr. 11, West Germany

- SHANTI SHILA, P.O.Box 358 MCC, Makati Rizal, Philippines
  Tel: 70-33-14

- AKASH, 254 Payneham Rd., Joslin, Adelaide, South Australia 5034,
  Australia

- ASHEESH, c/o Oda, Kangawa-Ken, Chigasaki-Shi, Tomoe 2-8-23,
  Japan

- ANAND NEED, P.O.Box 72424, Nairobi Kenya, East Africa

- PURNAM, Caixa Postal 1946, Porto Alegre—R.G.Sul, Brazil
  Tel: 21888